PRAISE FOR *Strength*

"I found myself underlining something interesting or revelatory on every page. It was refreshing to read a book about autism that was naturally infused with positivity. So much of what I loved was what was left out – no stereotypical autism, no pathologising language, no disheartening perspectives and the like. [*Strength Not Deficit*] presents autism as it is for so many of us – something that shapes every corner of our lives and enhances all that we do. It sparked so many thoughts and I will surely be returning to each section I underlined to reflect deeper."

*Jackie Schuld, Autistic Writer and
Art Therapist specialising in Late Identified Autism*

"Having already read *The Umbrella Picker*, it was of little surprise to me that every chapter of *Strength Not Deficit* was peppered with wisdom and insight of the kind that only the combination of autistic obsession and lived experience can bring! I've no doubt it will be invaluable to those on their own journey of discovery."

Hayley Graham, Consultant Child & Adolescent Psychotherapist

"We are always in need of more stories that will inspire people and help spur them on as they ready themselves to take the plunge into the high-stakes world of entrepreneurialism. Getting a business up and running from scratch can be an incredibly daunting task – no matter your aptitude or level of experience – and it's not always easy to see the light at the end of the tunnel.

"With *Strength Not Deficit*, author and accomplished entrepreneur Jane McNeice offers a refreshingly positive outlook that is sure to motivate any aspiring businessperson and fill them with the confidence they need to succeed.

"Challenging ablest views and societal stigmas, her story illustrates that Autism needn't be an obstacle to overcome in business and that, on the contrary, it can be a real advantage. Yet while her experiences are undoubtedly specific, the lessons gleaned from them can be applied to anyone who has a goal that they are trying to achieve."

Daniel Fell, CEO at Doncaster Chamber.

STRENGTH not DEFICIT BECAUSE I am Autistic!

Exposing the common Autistic traits with the power to overcome challenge, leading to achievement and success...

... and what happens when that success is met with ableism.

Jane McNeice

First published in 2024 by Fuzzy Flamingo
Copyright © Jane McNeice 2024

Jane McNeice has asserted her right to be identified as the author of this Work in accordance with the Copyright, Designs and Patents Act 1988.

ISBN: 978-1-7393669-7-1

All rights reserved.
No part of this publication may be reproduced, stored in a retrieval system, or transmitted in any form or by any means, electronic, mechanical, photocopying, recording or otherwise, without the prior permission of the copyright owner.

Editing and design by Fuzzy Flamingo
www.fuzzyflamingo.co.uk

Cover and author photos © 2022 Collette Evans,
Picture Perfect Photography
https://www.pictureperfectphoto.co.uk/

A catalogue for this book is available from the British Library.

*For my late brother Robert who put 'ability' at the heart of dis**ability** and proved all the naysayers wrong!*
We miss your dearly every single day.
Sis xx

DISCLAIMER

This book has been written to provide information and motivation for exploration by readers. It is sold with the understanding that the Author is not engaged to render any type of psychological, legal, business, or other kind of professional advice. The content of each chapter is the sole expression and opinion of its Author. Do not use this book to diagnose or develop a treatment plan for a health problem, condition, or disease without consulting a qualified care provider. No warranties or guarantees are expressed or implied by the Author. The Author shall not be liable for any physical, psychological, emotional, financial, or commercial damages, including, but not limited to, special, accidental, consequential or other damage. You are responsible for your own choices, actions and results.

Where the Work of others has been referenced, the Author has made every effort to ensure that the source is identified through appropriate citation. If you believe a piece of Work has been omitted, or has been cited incorrectly, the Author will be pleased to make the appropriate acknowledgements or revisions in any future edition.

Some names and identification details have been changed to protect the privacy of individuals.

NOTE FOR READERS

The author uses a capital A in Autism when diagnosed, a small a when undiagnosed.

Contents

	Prologue	xi
1:	The Suffering Years	1
2:	My Journey to the Truth: Actually Autistic!	13
3:	It Ain't Over Till It's Over	29
4:	A Variant Not a Fault!	40
5:	Obsess about It, and You'll be Successful at It!	66
6:	Making Something from Nothing; Ignoring the Naysayers and Autistic Perseverance	100
7:	All Ideas Are Borne Inside Our Heads	125
8:	Being Organised and Efficient with Working Memory Problems	138
9:	Social Masking and the Ability to Adapt Quickly	151
10:	People Pleasing and the Empathy Advantage	161
11:	No One Way of Communicating	175
12:	Gaining a Corporate Edge through ~~Fortune-telling~~ Pattern Seeking	186
13:	Anxiety: Harnessing the Power of Discomfort	192
14:	Self-care for All Business Owners, Especially for Autistic Ones!	198
	Epilogue	211
	Acknowledgements	225
	Endnotes	229

Prologue

After my life went topsy-turvy on the 22nd of June 2021, a taunting yet enlightening thought persistently took residence...

> *"Why can the bumblebee fly? Because no one told it that it could not."*

Many have subscribed to the myth that the cumbersome bumblebee defies all laws of physics and aerodynamics in its ability to fly. This stems from the work of French Entomologist August Magnan who asserted that the bumblebee's ability to do so was scientifically impossible. Debunked by the fact that the bumblebee *does actually fly* (and other research), we simply know it *is* possible, but nevertheless that notion must have found its way into my subconscious and chose to reveal itself to my conscious mind at the most opportune time for me to take solace in it. Its personal message: **Believe the impossible, you've been your own living proof!**

★ ★ ★

STRENGTH *not* DEFECIT

Have you ever cut yourself and not noticed the pain until you see the wound? Have you ever been so consumed by distraction that it just makes you *forget* the pain and your surroundings? When we are not alert to something, something limiting, then it often doesn't affect us. It's as if it doesn't exist.

For a long time, I had no limits, not until someone told me I had a condition, a disorder, which *can* limit, and that I had done phenomenally well despite this. Overcoming the limits, I was told, is very challenging. But I knew that already because I *had* in fact overcome so much. How? I just wasn't aware that limits existed for me any more or less than they existed for anyone else.

Today I see the bumblebee message as an early warning sign, a warning not to internalise the limits set on me and my people by the outside world, or what others think *should* be our limits and our abilities. We ourselves define these, individually, not others for us. The challenge? Others need to be aware of that fact too…

CHAPTER 1

The Suffering Years

To describe a life-changing diagnosis as 'topsy-turvy change' doesn't even come close to qualifying it. No words feel sufficient to describe what a life-changing diagnosis can do to a person. Some people view diagnoses purely as labels, to be defined by, or not. Some people reject them, some people accept them, and some totally and utterly embrace them. I totally and utterly embrace my Autism diagnosis, and yes, I do allow it to totally define me and who I am. Why? Because I searched a lifetime for it. I lived undiagnosed autistic for forty-five years, half of my life, that is assuming I'm being optimistic about my future. For me, it is now the lens through which *everything* is viewed, past, present and future.

Like many Autistics, my long-term memory is superior to most people's memory recall and my first memory is of around eighteen months to two years of age. I was playing with my three-year older brother Robert on a wooden play frame at a small Methodist church playgroup in Thorne, the small town in Yorkshire where I grew up. I remember climbing, parking my little bottom on the wooden slide, and gliding down. It was enjoyable, and I felt safe! Sadly, that feeling of 'safe' was short-lived.

As I reflect today, I recognise how precious that memory is – it is the only memory I have where I totally feel safe, and it is precious because I was with my mum and my older brother Robert who is sadly no longer with us. From the age of three and the time when I commenced nursery school, I started to feel something else, another emotion. It wasn't familiar or comforting, and it most definitely was not 'safe'. It was fear, ebbing and flowing around me all of the time. I would seek solace, reassurance and as much comfort as possible in the arms of my mum, but everything else was just frightening, and most frightening of all… was people!

To this day, 20th July 2023, that feeling hasn't *ever* gone away. I don't know what it's like to wake up not feeling scared, not feeling it in the pit of my stomach, and not having to manage the physically disabling challenges that go with it – in the main, gastrointestinal challenges. My anxiety is not neurosis, it is not episodic, I am never symptom free, and there is a strong likelihood (and acceptance on my part) that I won't ever be. But today I am fortunate in that I know *why* I experience those feelings.

The physical gastric challenges that go with my anxiety are disabling and these were the first motivator that encouraged me to visit my GP in respect of my mental health as a teen, and so a diagnosis of irritable bowel syndrome (IBS) soon followed. Intervention after intervention was used to try and manage this hidden and embarrassing health problem I was living with, a physical health problem linked to my mental health. Thinking back, I tried medication – several medications, in fact – exercise, dietary change, self-help books, alternative therapies, including acupuncture, and Bowen therapy. You name it, I will have given it a go. That alone was tiring. It led in the end to extreme dietary management, and a logical (my logic that is) decision to reduce and nearly stop eating combined with over exercising. In reality, the very makings of a serious eating disorder! If food didn't go in, or was used for energy, then it couldn't go out, could it? Black or white thinking at its best.

> Note: Black or white, or 'all or nothing' thinking, while described as a 'distorted thought pattern'[1] in the principals of cognitive behavioural therapy, is normal for Autistics, as is ruminative thinking – repetitive thoughts going over and over the same thing. These are some of the many examples of neurotypical thinking imposed upon neurodivergent people like me, suggesting our way of thinking is wrong, rather than different. We like facts, they are black and white, and predictable. We like logic and we are logical! Ruminative thinking also serves a purpose in that it allows us to process the complex social experiences and different ways we experience the world, and it helps us to problem solve and work out solutions for the future. Second note: A strong need for control is also something many Autistics experience and is linked to the world being very unpredictable and confusing for us. We tend to

> control as much as we possibly can to ease that discomfort. I will rule out as many of the unknowns as can be ruled out based on my sphere of control. I was controlling my food intake because I had no sense of control over my bodily functions and the social anxiety I was experiencing, despite having tried everything. This was my ultimate last control. I had nothing left. Third note: An individual risk factor for eating disorders is a strong need to be in control.[2] Fourth note: Conditions such as IBS are also a risk factor for developing disordered eating, which, if more severe, could lead to an eating disorder.[3] Autistic people are thought to represent around 37% of people with anorexia nervosa, but this is likely to be higher due to the under-diagnosis of Autism in girls, women, trans and non-binary people.[4]

Fortunately, before the consequences of my behaviour manifested severely, my GP offered a prescription for a drug called dihydrocodeine, one of the opioid family of drugs, a strong and quickly absorbing painkiller whose side effects are peristalsis (constipation), among other things. This medication would slow down my over-active bowel that I never quite felt I had control over, and which was causing me panic attacks, heightened anxiety and to totally obsess over my bodily functions constantly. If nothing else, the medication would provide a cessation to *that* unwanted obsession as well as the uncontrollable symptoms. These symptoms had been plaguing my life since adolescence, and continually worsened until they were uncontrollable and were taking me very close to a serious eating disorder and suicide.

> Note: Gastrointestinal problems are a very common comorbid/co-existing condition in those who are Autistic,[5] though the exact reason is unclear. My belief, in my own case, is that they are inextricably linked to my comorbid anxiety, which in turn is linked to my being Autistic and the myriad issues surrounding that fact.

The gastric problems were my nemesis, and unfortunately, the gastric problems did not operate alone. My gastric problems had a sidekick, a co-conspirator, and that was the anxiety, the very same anxiety that had started at the age of three and continues today. The gastric symptoms I had identified were the first symptom that motivated me to go and see my GP, which is often the case with mental illness. It is the physical symptoms we seek help for *before* we seek help for the psychological symptoms. We tend to have a greater awareness of the symptoms of physical ill health than mental ill health, and GPs tend to explore the physical symptoms first, which in the case of mental illness, often results in not finding anything organically wrong with the person, as was the case with me. I'd had all the tests, including the invasive and degrading endoscopies – gastroscopy and colonoscopy, both in the same day on one occasion! Then attention is given to the person's psychological health. Our failure to recognise and acknowledge the mind/body relationship blinds us to the fact that both are related in any case. My belief is that, by raising mental health awareness and literacy in society, we can improve understanding here, which is where my working life and business comes in. My own symptoms were most definitely of mind *and* body, it was more a case of just how much each was contributing to the other, but ultimately both needed addressing for my survival.

In 2003, my mental ill health peaked, the symptoms being at their most acute level. It was year one of my undergraduate degree, and I was pushing myself harder and harder to achieve the highest grades on record. No limits, remember. If 100% existed, then surely that mark could be achieved, or why would the grade range be 0–100%? Black and white logic. I had received 100% on a European law exam in AS level Law the year previous, so I could surely match that again. But off-the-charts determination and high achievement has its price. Its price is burnout, mental ill health, physical ill health and yes, of course, *all* are linked.

> Note: Autistics are statistically more prone to burning out than Allistics (non-Autistic people), typically referred to as Autistic burnout,[6] and Autistic burnout is a disabling whole-body experience.

My anxiety had reached a level that my mood was now in the gutter, but I could not stop what I wanted to achieve. Like a car being driven at 100 miles an hour into a wall, I was still motivated and still foot flat to the floor! I had started to fantasise about dying and an end to it all, the pain was becoming more than I could cope with, and my coping mechanism seemed to be to keep driving faster and faster, metaphorically speaking. The thoughts had become active rather than passive suicidal thoughts. I knew how I would end my life. But I also had the foresight to know that this was a sign I needed help, and fortunately I had the *will* to survive – the life connection still louder than that which was drawing me towards death – and enough confidence and verbal skill to articulate my need for help. As I write that, I worry about the person today who doesn't have those protective factors and is feeling the way I felt at the time.

I was still connected to life. I went to see my GP. It was a life-preserving decision to do so. My GP prescribed me sertraline, a type of drug belonging to the SSRI (selective serotonin reuptake inhibitor) family of medications, often prescribed for common mental health conditions like anxiety and depressive disorders, and gave me a diagnosis of generalised anxiety disorder, an anxiety disorder characterised by excessive worry over a long period of time (at least six months for diagnosis) and which has an impact on day-to-day living. This would not be the only mental illness I would be diagnosed with in my lifetime. In 2019, I would also receive a diagnosis of social anxiety (also known as social phobia), as the outcome of going to see a private psychiatrist because of a belief I had a personality disorder. Some Autistic women will in fact receive a misdiagnosis of a personality disorder prior to them being identified as, or diagnosed, Autistic. It is commonly the personality disorder referred to as BPD (borderline personality disorder), sometimes diagnosed as EUPD (emotionally unstable personality disorder), though my belief was that I had OCPD (obsessive compulsive personality disorder), which is a different personality disorder.

> Note: EUPD/BPD is a common misdiagnosis, particularly in women, prior to an Autism diagnosis.[7] Many late diagnosed Autistics will seek to have this diagnosis rescinded afterwards due to issues surrounding stigma and other negative impacts. The diagnosis has been criticised on many levels, including the stigma and treatment of people with the diagnosis, and its use as a 'holding diagnosis' that says more about the knowledge of the diagnostician than the symptoms of the patient. Anecdotally, I vividly recall a conversation in 2016 with a mental health practitioner who asserted, "They give BPD when they don't know what's wrong with you."

Obsessive compulsive personality disorder is a personality disorder also, but different to the more commonly known mental health condition obsessive compulsive disorder (OCD), which is an anxiety disorder, a neurosis, *not* a personality disorder. Most people do not go searching for personality disorders or a personality disorder diagnosis. Personality disorders are some of the most stigmatised of all mental health conditions, and people tend to be given them, rather than search for them. On reflection, the very fact I was seeking this out is testimony to my need for my truth, regardless of what the truth was. I would have dealt with any stigma later. It's not uncommon for women in particular to be misdiagnosed with a variety of mental illnesses prior to them being diagnosed Autistic. Misdiagnosis in this group is high. It is very important to say, however, that you can have either, both, and none, they are not mutually exclusive. They very often co-exist, but you can also have one of these mental health conditions and *not* be Autistic. It's just that Autistic people tend to have a lot of comorbid illnesses, including mental illnesses.

The GP at the time did not refer me for talking therapies as I was already receiving counselling for recurrent water infections caused by stress – *quelle surprise*! The signs were all there and *always* had been. The connections were simply not being made due to a lack of information about non-stereotypical Autism in girls (Autism awareness) on the part of so many – including me, ultimately – it was as simple as that. This is one of the fundamental issues why so many people live undiagnosed and suffering for so long. Few people have been sufficiently Autism aware, and for a very long time the information has been centred around outdated stereotypes of Autism, with very little quality information and awareness of Autism in girls, and particularly non-stereotypical Autism. The science and research about Autism in girls is also left wanting, which compounds this further. Thankfully that is changing, and when awareness is greater and this information is freely available and accessible to those who are lost and suffering, they will make their own connection, just like I did. It's not rocket science!

I took the prescribed medication for a year, initially feeling spaced out, and wanting so much to believe that it was working, and that I was 'getting better'. I wanted to believe the counselling was also working, and that I wasn't just placating the counsellor that she was providing a successful intervention. My inability *not* to 'people please' made me want to make her happy and to be grateful for her time and effort. After a year, it all slowly came to an end, because I had tricked myself and the professionals into thinking that it was working. I slowly came off the medication, and slowly retracted myself from the crutch that had been my Monday morning counselling, which had conveniently excused me from the mandatory end of lecture presentation I had to deliver in my criminology degree module 'Representing Crime'. Getting out of *that* was lifesaving in and of itself! It was a time in my life when I had no voice, no public voice that is, but that did not mean I had nothing to say. I simply wanted to hide away, and in no way wanted to speak in front of my peers, let alone stand up in front of the classroom with gastric problems and do it! Would you if you could not control your anxious over-active digestive system? Mmmm, you are hearing me now, I'm sure. But nothing had changed in respect of my mental health and my gastric troubles. I was just fooling myself it had improved because that is what I so badly wanted to believe, and because I didn't want to hurt anyone else's feelings. The counselling just left me feeling that all the blame sat with a family member for all my troubles, which was not exclusively the case.

My life was a perennial cycle of managing anxiety, depression, gastric problems, burnout and suicidal thoughts, with therapeutic interventions thrown in as and when it all got too much, again. The circumstances of my life and how it was playing out just emphasised to me that I was no good at anything, no good at this thing we call life! I felt a failure in all sense of the word, and my self-worth was on the floor, despite trying so hard to be someone of value. Several people, including my line manager at work several years before my diagnosis, had highlighted just how self-critical I was; she too could see my low self-worth. Today, I see it as the undiagnosed autistic narrative, illustrating very low self-esteem, and present in many of us who have suffered for being missed, and who have always felt inadequate at life and never good enough at our roles in life. When we get diagnosed Autistic (if we are fortunate enough) we learn that wasn't our truth at all. We reframe everything because we learn, by nature of what we have been living through, we *were* in fact bloody great survivors and resilient too! Learning we are Autistic helps to flip the script and to reframe the narrative. We see ourselves and our life history through a totally new lens, an Autistic one, rather than the incorrect neurotypical one we had been using previously! We stop using neurotypical ideals, and instead work out our own Autistic ideals and measures of happiness, well-being and success, and just like us, *they too* are different.

At this point, my health issues were a challenge, and I sought solace in the form of things I had been doing for a long time – reading, academia and learning, motherhood, and in the identity that my career provided. To others, I looked successful and okay.

I had become a mum at the age of nineteen, which provided its own identity, but there was still a pervasive sense that I did not belong or fit in as a mother amongst other mothers. Motherhood is an acceptable identity in our society, unless you become one too early, too late, or not at all, which society will often judge, especially in the absence of the full story (and sometimes even with it). Motherhood did not fill the gaping void I was feeling, and no matter how much I loved my child, it did not change that fact. So, I then sought identity as a student, and ultimately, I *did* achieve my goal, delivering on the high expectations I had placed upon myself in year one of my undergraduate degree, when three years later I graduated with first class honours (in all modules from year one to year three). A part of me always felt that if I *just* achieve this, I *will* be good enough. It was almost my pre-diagnosis mantra… If I *just* do this, or if I just *have* this, or if I could just *be* this… If I met the milestones that represented 'normal' and achieved them at a higher level than everyone else (the 'normal'), then I would convince society (and myself) of my normality. I'd be accepted by the herd, and I would fit in. I'd be okay.

But I was never okay; nothing I did or achieved made me feel good enough. Not until that fateful day on the 22nd of June 2021…

CHAPTER 2

My Journey to the Truth: Actually Autistic!

I should firstly say that it's not uncommon that when a parent identifies their child is autistic, or the parent seeks or receives an autism diagnosis for their child, they too start to work out that they are autistic, and so too comes their own diagnosis. This isn't a million miles from what happened to our family. That isn't to say that *all* parents of Autistic children will also be Autistic, but there is a strong statistical likelihood they will be. Research suggests Autism is up to 83% genetic, with one of the biological parents likely being Autistic too.[8]

During Covid-19 lockdown one, we were experiencing behavioural challenges with our six-year-old son. The reality is we had been experiencing them for the previous four and a half years, but we hadn't yet joined the dots or made any connections. Not only did a lack of Autism awareness blind me to my own Autism, but it also blinded me to my children's. I didn't yet have a neurotypically brained comparator amongst my children that would alert me to the vast differences in the three of them. Our six-year-old was my husband's first child and, as it turned out, I had only raised undiagnosed autistic children up to that point – one undiagnosed autistic child – and, of course, as an undiagnosed autistic myself. I thought *everyone* experienced the same parenting challenges I had, and it was more a case that *I* just wasn't any good at it – echoes of the lost girl narrative again.

During the Covid lockdowns, like many parents and carers, we had a pronounced length of undivided time with our children, which would not have been afforded otherwise. By then, I had given birth to our youngest child, who we believe is neurotypical – the comparator. I say that today with some hesitation, as I cannot 100% rule out that Ben isn't neurodivergent and that we are not, once again, simply overlooking the connections or that related issues have not yet revealed themselves. I am open-minded.

On reflection, for all of us, it was at the age of seven that we all started to reveal the more noticeable signs we were neurodivergent. Ben is now seven and I have quite a few moments currently where tiny red flags and questions emerge, particularly when he displays extreme emotional responses. Questions around the presence of ADHD (attention deficit hyperactivity disorder) but not Autism. ADHD was my blind spot too. I am alert to Autism but less so to ADHD traits, though this is changing, fast. At seven, Ben is a phenomenal computer gamer and, according to his self-taught IT support business owner and computer gaming father, he is displaying excellence in computer gaming that is superior to many adults, including his own gaming skills, and this has been the case since Ben was four years old. I would not have a clue, as this is totally outside of my interests, other than vicarious interest through them both. Contrary to ideas that all Autistics are good at tech, I am not. I am adequate at best. I have sufficient knowledge for my work, and knowing anything beyond that is of little interest to me and a waste of brain space I would prefer to use elsewhere. While it is well documented and acknowledged that there is a disproportionate number of diagnosed and undiagnosed autistics working in the tech industry, I believe this has created a dominant stereotype and consequent blind spot preventing acknowledgement of all the Autistics *successfully* working outside of this field. I believe there is a disproportionately high number of undiagnosed autistics working in the 'helping industries', for example, as much as in STEM (science, tech, engineering, maths), which I will talk more about later in the book.

My subtle concerns about Ben could also be an indicator of an over alertness to neurodivergence, and I am equally alert to confirmation bias. As it stands currently, he is not *significantly* suffering or disabled by anything that is present, so we have no reason to act, yet. My concern with Ben is that a label at the moment may in fact have a reverse and damaging effect because of society's prejudices. I am protecting him from this until I cannot. Currently he is achieving well in life and school, and I don't want society's ableism to change that through an ADHD label. We are observing closely for substantial change, and if at any point the suffering begins to outweigh the cost of ableism, then we will act. At the moment, we are 'watchfully waiting'. As for describing my youngest son as 'the comparator', Ben is, of course, so much more than a comparator! People are often quick to deter child comparison, but had we not produced a neurotypical child (or child with a different neurotype, as it may turn out), we may not have noticed the stark differences in our two boys. I didn't know anything other than raising Autistic children. I just thought *all* parents had it tough and all children presented challenges, but we weren't experiencing these challenges at the time with Ben, our youngest.

I had already raised my now grown-up daughter, Laura, who was twenty-five in 2020, and we did not yet know she too was autistic. My two eldest children presented the same; Oliver, currently, and on reflection, Laura when she was a child. It was our youngest Ben who highlighted to us that there was something very different in my first two children that wasn't visible in our third. My husband is not the biological father of my eldest child.

After a seismic 'meltdown' (which we now preferably refer to as emotional dysregulation) in my eldest son, which at the time we regarded as a ten on the zero-to-ten 'melt-o-meter', my husband, after tapping away on his keyboard for a few minutes, looked up and said, "Jane, I think Oliver has ADHD." I am an open-minded person, but still the idea felt discomfiting, although I also sensed a truism in what my husband said. In hindsight, the research and comment were illustrative of my own and my husband's stereotyped thinking at the time… challenging behaviour we would have described as 'naughty', therefore he must have ADHD. For that I apologise to anyone reading this who has ADHD. I now know better. Little did we know that comment would be the very first step we would take on our path to neuro-enlightenment for the whole of our family!

Within days, I had spoken to the GP and to the special educational needs co-ordinator (SENCO) at my son's school. Much like when seeking my own health interventions, there was a sense I was a fraud, fraudulent in terms of my own needs, and the same feeling when trying to explain the challenges we were experiencing with our son. I always felt that I was slightly over-exaggerating or catastrophising and that there were others far worse off than me. For a long time, I was gaslighting myself, dismissing myself from the truth, and invalidating my painful experiences. This sense of fraud I still experience today, for myself and with my Autistic son, and the same with Ben, where I am questioning if I am overreacting in thinking he has ADHD. I worry greatly that school and others will think I am just 'label hunting', adding to the unfortunate narrative we currently hear: "There wasn't any of this ADHD and Autism in our day!"

Thankfully, the GP was sufficiently satisfied with my concerns about Oliver to refer on, and within a few months, we received a response letter from the local Children and Adolescent Mental Health Service (CAMHS) detailing a list of requirements before anything further could be done, and highlighting that assessment was not in fact carried out by them. Most actions centred around ensuring our parenting skills were up to scratch. For example, we were instructed to attend a Webster-Stratton training course before any next steps could be taken, and to seek an Early Help referral. I've since learned (and experienced) that the parent-blaming rhetoric is both historical and current around parents of neurodivergent children. Many parents report having experienced this. Go back a few generations and the so-called 'refrigerator mother'[9] was the reason for Autistic boys (because back then no one believed girls could *be* Autistic, otherwise said mother would probably have been held responsible for their Autism too). This, amongst many other examples, is just more evidence of female oppression. Steve Silberman's book *Neurotribes*[10] catalogues this and a myriad of blaming and historical atrocities towards Autistics and those raising them. It's still happening today, perhaps less overtly, but it most definitely still exists.

The saddest indication of this is the many parents accused of FII (fabricated or induced illness), otherwise known as Munchausen by proxy, when they raise concerns about related health issues and/or neurodivergence. There are a frighteningly growing number of cases where parents of neurodivergent children have had children removed from their care by overzealous local authorities, another form of state sanctioned bullying of parents of neurodivergent children.

It wasn't long before I was feeling disenchanted and impatient with 'the system'. My low tolerance for tardiness and inefficient systems didn't help. We were, as we know it today, the lucky ones, able to pursue assessment through private means. It was not cheap, still took longer than expected, but it most definitely was worth it. So off we went, down a different pathway towards the same outcome where either route would have led us, simply at different points in time.

Many Autistics, and parents of Autistics, will talk about the benefits of peer support, other parents and carers, online forums and support groups. For our family, they have been some of the most beneficial supporters, and our most impassioned allies. One such ally, a mother at my son's school, pointed me in the direction of a parenting supporting group on Facebook called Sunshine Support CIC, which I still recommend to other parents (https://sunshine-support.org/). As I so often do, I thought, *Oh I will look at that*, and then forgot till I remembered due to my poor working memory.

> Note: Autistics often experience executive dysfunction issues, including working memory (short-term memory) problems.[11]

I eventually remembered to check out the link one Saturday morning while cyber-loafing in bed, brew in one hand, phone in the other. I clicked on the page, scrolled down, and came across a post which stopped me in my tracks and caused me to weep with joy and relief. The post was titled 'Girls with Autism'. Shared by Sunshine Support CIC, the post had twenty traits illustrated as a mind-map, a visual. Those twenty traits were:

- Creative talents, e.g., artistic, love of writing, musical.
- May appear shy.
- Practises conversations in mind.
- Escapes through imagination.
- Trusting.
- May talk a LOT about favourite topics.
- May appear young for her age.
- Adopts behaviour in order to fit in.
- Enjoys spending time alone.
- Unusual eye contact.
- Anxiety.
- OCD tendencies.
- Routine is important to her.
- Dislike of conflict.
- Perfectionist.
- May feel out of place in the world.
- Unique sense of humour.
- Unsure when it's her turn to talk.
- Loves animals.
- Sensitive.

I read the points and sobbed. I had self-identified I was autistic, and my own search was finally over after forty-four years.

I then did what many an *actually* Autistic person would do… I scribed all the items as headings, rated them between one and ten points each (ten being the highest), wrote down my rationale for my meeting each trait and conducted a pseudo-self-assessment of my female autistic traits. I used all points, including the first point as four individual items. There are twenty-three in total. My pseudo-self-assessment resulted in a score of 219/230, and this was as objective as I could achieve at this stage. I scored lowest on love of animals, in the main because my fear and anxiety around animals often gets in the way of my love for them – the heightened autistic trait in one area simply nulling another. The very fact that I undertook this process was telling of my autistic brain type.

My search had ended, but my self-identification now needed to be clinically diagnosed. Why? Well, a year earlier, I had 'barked up the wrong tree' thinking I had OCPD, and as you will recall, the very qualified psychiatrist told me I was wrong. What if I was wrong again? My right brain, the creative side of my brain, linked to my heart, my gut, and the wider universe, knew I was right, that I was autistic, and that I had finally found myself. Right brain had already started its own celebration party with music and [silent] party poppers. But my serious logical left brain, who is often more dominant and overshadows my right brain, stepped forward, turned the music down, and said, "No, no, no, hold your horses, just you wait a minute, Jane McNeice! You went to see that *expert* last year, thinking you had a personality disorder, and he told you that you were wrong! How do you *know* you are *not* wrong again!?" Undeterred, my right brain stepped equally forward, and simply said,

"Let's do this," proceeded to turn the music back up and continued her one-woman celebration party.

I had no choice. For me, a formal diagnosis was important. I don't like woolly or vague, I want concrete fact, rather than to be left guessing. I am also of the opinion that a formal diagnosis can assist further with support, but note well, it in no way *guarantees* it, as my family has learned all too well. Without a diagnosis, Autistics can face further scrutiny and disbelief, questioning, and proof seeking from others – friends, family, employers, statutory services. If you are okay with that, then that is fine, but I wasn't. I think this relates to the fact that I had always felt fraudulent about my challenges and symptoms, so to have someone question my judgement would simply have affirmed any fraudulent thinking that I was having. The fraudulent thinking is in fact now proving itself to have been Autism related, faulty, not reflective of the truth, and is something many late diagnosed Autistics have experienced.

Few people have questioned my clinical diagnosis, but there was definite scepticism prior to diagnosis, the time between self-identification and the formal Autism assessment. The shorter the period between the two the better as far as I was concerned. This is just one of many challenges people in the UK face when they are on an NHS waiting list left an unacceptably long time for assessment. That is just one of many things that needs to change.

Today, I would add another critically important reason to have a full and proper Autism assessment. While self-identified autistic people remain in that space, which of course is absolutely their choice, they will be missed from some of the statistics, and each and every one of these numbers matters. They matter, a lot. If people are missed from statistics, society is not seeing the truest picture of Autism, and statutory services are being absolved of the need to support us. Each number that is missed gives the authorities permission to discount us when calculating budgets for financial support and when commissioning services, because they will often focus on the diagnosed Autistics, not the hidden ones who may not be recorded on any 'systems', especially if they have not disclosed formally. We make it very easy for statutory services to say, "Well, there are only XXXX many Autistics in this borough therefore we only need this much budget or service," and so *all* autistics lose out on much needed support. While there are lots of other known barriers, I do wonder if some autistics might not choose the next step of formal assessment due to fear, fear that they may be wrong, the very same fear I had. My belief is that most won't be in nearly all cases, which the research supports,[12] but it is an understandable fear in those who have been desperately searching for an answer to 'why', especially when they think they have finally found it. It's a fear I fully relate to and one I sat uncomfortably with for a year between self-identification and clinical diagnosis. If the assessor had told me I wasn't Autistic, that I had been wrong, that I hadn't found my truth, I literally do not know what I would have done. There would have been such a huge sense of loss that I don't know how I would have lived with it or if I could have. So, you can see why every step in a journey towards diagnosis is an incredibly huge and challenging one for each of us.

In reality, I knew that very Saturday morning in 2021 that I was autistic, and that morning was the start of my own journey towards formal diagnosis. I didn't really need more evidence in respect of myself, I knew I was autistic, but I was still not qualified to self-diagnose, instead only to self-identify, and I needed the *actual* proof. I owe my parent-friend and Sunshine Support CIC an eternal debt of gratitude for their assisting me to find myself, without which I would likely have remained lost and overlooked forever, or at least lost for a few more years. I do think eventually the right information would have crossed my path, a second, or a third chance to 'connect'. Perhaps on a spiritual level, I believe I was meant to find out when I was forty-four, for reasons that are beyond me, reasons that only something bigger than me knows. My own spiritual belief is that my forty-four years of pain were in some way purposeful. Someone somewhere thought I needed to experience sufficient pain to fuel the fire that would (and I write this with great hope) create positive change for others who are suffering in just the same way I had been. It's the kind of fire which motivates me to go back and to help the rest, the others still lost and suffering, and to write this book, for example. Please don't interpret that as delusions of grandeur or a messiah complex, it is merely my desire to make a difference, ease suffering and to be a worthwhile human being. You will, I'm sure, make of it what you will, based on your own thinking and beliefs. I am just sharing a snapshot of my own, something that has helped me to process my past.

As you will see in my own journey towards Autism diagnosis, social media was fundamental. It provided the conduit for the information that would cause me to self-identify – social media saved my life. Love or loathe social media – I know it can divide people – for many of us it has removed a blind spot. It has given us Autism awareness. Social media has in part bridged the gap between the non-identified and identified; it has given us the missing piece we had been searching for.

I firmly believe there are three core conditions required for self-identification to occur:

1. self-awareness
2. a searching or receptiveness to an explanation not yet known, and
3. Autism awareness (including non-stereotypical).

I had the first two of these conditions in abundance. I had turned myself inside out in terms of self-awareness. I had been desperately searching for myself for forty-four years, but unfortunately, I was still distinctly lacking number three – non-stereotypical Autism awareness information. The moment I saw this – a social media post of less than ninety words – I worked it out in less than sixty seconds! Today, as I see it, my life's purpose, or as the Japanese would say, my *ikigai* – reason for being – is to put that information (number three) in front of as many people as possible, for as long as I'm functioning, so that others who have numbers one and two, but are missing number three – those who are autistic but do not yet know it – will work it out for themselves when the last blind spot is removed. It is now my life's purpose. I didn't choose it; it has chosen me.

Why is this needed? Because, as my family's experience attests, the 'system' is very ill equipped to find us (more on that in the next chapter), especially if we are female, especially if we are high achievers (the hidden and last to be found, so often will be), and especially if we are exceptional social maskers. More on that later.

As for social media being good or bad, the evidence base doesn't substantiate much either way, because it's hard to say. We all use different platforms, have different exposure times, different newsfeeds, and threads, so we can't measure like with like. I glance at my husband's social media newsfeed and think, *Engine parts and cars – *yawn* – uninteresting for me!* He would look at my newsfeed and think, *Autism and neurodivergence – *even bigger yawn* – uninteresting for me!* What excites him doesn't excite me and vice versa. Which one is good or bad? Either and neither. When I am training people to support other people's mental health in my work, especially when they are supporting young people, I simply encourage them to always take a 'person-centred' approach. This might look like encouraging the supporter to ask, "Do you use social media? Could that be influencing how you feel today? Yes? Oh, okay, shall we have a think about things that might improve that, such as less screen time, or dialling down the notifications? How would you feel about that?" Another person in need might respond, "Oh no, social media helps me to feel better. I am part of an online community who offer me support and…" It really does depend on each situation, and a person-centred approach allows flexibility for each.

And so it was, on the 22nd of June 2021, I entered The Counselling Room in Hemel Hempstead, where a qualified Autism assessor told me, within five minutes of being in the room(!), that I was Autistic. She had read all the paperwork I had submitted prior to the assessment, read the blogs I had written on my business website, explored the detailed biographical history, and was sufficiently confident of my neurotype. Nevertheless, she dutifully followed the due process, my diagnosis was agreed by the assessor and seconded by a qualified psychiatrist. A week or so later, I received the detailed report, my Autism diagnosis written out in black and white, verified by the psychiatrist, and with an additional suggestion that I also had the condition dyscalculia. My GCSE grade E maths, amongst other numbers-based challenges, without doubt supports that finding. My junior school maths teacher would most definitely have endorsed the finding, since he used to give me pity marks for just putting my name on the test paper!

I find it hard to convey to anyone what that moment of truth felt like. I use analogies of it being like winning the lottery or being told you are no longer terminal. Only those exposed to something so life-changingly positive could even get close to knowing that feeling. My diagnosis did not take away the gastric problems or the anxiety, that suffering remains, but it has made every single experience of my past and present understandable and explainable, to myself and to others. Now I know 'why' I am, and that is *everything* to me!

My name is Jane McNeice, and I say with pride, discovery and good fortune that **I am Autistic**.

CHAPTER 3

It Ain't Over Till It's Over

My journey ended as it did because we had noticed something different in our son. His behaviour was in fact the start of our journey, and his journey was ongoing alongside my own journey to diagnosis. My own and my son's journeys towards the truth weren't the only two that were happening during this time; a third, my daughter's, was also unfolding in front of our eyes.

I talk more about the unfolding of our family's journey to Autism diagnosis in my memoir *The Umbrella Picker*, so I don't want to simply repeat that story here, and I am in danger of easily doing so. As an Autistic, I will easily go off on a tangent and get so impassioned about what I am thinking that I will be off down a rabbit hole never to be seen again; all very *Alice in Wonderland*! That said, I think it would be helpful to tell you a little more about our family's history, so you have the fullest context.

Raising my daughter Laura felt incredibly difficult. I constantly felt, as I did with Oliver, my second child, that I simply was rubbish at motherhood and that everyone else had it worked out. Nothing I ever did quite felt good enough, no matter how hard I tried. I was a mother walking on eggshells so that Laura didn't 'kick off' when she couldn't have things her own way and could never fathom why when we bought her ice cream it would be cornet erect on the floor twenty seconds later. As a toddler, she would rarely walk, and we would carry her everywhere, her dad nicknaming her 'Tiny Tim' like the Dickens character from *A Christmas Carol*. Reflecting today, I look back with shame and guilt. My living undiagnosed meant that my daughter was oppressed by my internalised ideals of both motherhood and childhood. I was raising and forcing her to be neurotypical. She was not. Just like me, she too was a square peg being forced any which way into a round hole and I was one of those forcing it. That was damaging for us both. When an adult is living undiagnosed, they will often suffer, perhaps not so much from the being missed, but the fact that by being missed we don't get the due support and flexibility that is needed. But what often goes unrecognised is that the offspring suffer that loss too. I oppressed my child, just the same way I had been oppressed by an undiagnosed autistic mum, who was and still is suffering (and undiagnosed), but today self-identifies as autistic. Mum's identification has only been the case since other family members have been diagnosed and her own non-stereotypical Autism awareness raised. She too was missing number three in the three conditions I identified that are required to self-identify autism, despite the fact that my late brother, her first born, was diagnosed Autistic, his additional learning disability revealing him early on in childhood. My daughter spent her childhood and youth feeling just the way I had and having many similar experiences. On reflection, we recognise she only ever had one or two friends, and they too were 'different', and she rarely received an invitation to any of her peers' birthday parties or celebrations.

Most notable of all, my daughter was [planned] pregnant at fifteen, and a mum at sixteen, searching desperately for some belonging and identity in motherhood, because she too was missing a huge part of herself. Just like I was and had been.

Just imagine for a moment how many 'professionals' move in on a family when their fifteen-year-old daughter becomes pregnant. We had a 'common assessment framework' in place, and regularly attended Team Around the Child (TAC) meetings. Around the table sat the school counsellor, a CAMHS cognitive behavioural therapist, a paediatric nurse from the Family Nurse Partnership, me, the high school head of year, and a family support worker from the local Sure Start children's centre. All had the potential to identify either of us, all failed to. None had sufficient non-stereotypical Autism awareness to be able to say, "Do you think these challenges could be explained by Laura being Autistic, or you an Autistic mum?" Never once did that happen for me or my children, not even an inference. At a conservative estimate, we have calculated, during our collective lifetimes to the point at which we were all diagnosed (my daughter, my son and myself), an exposure to well over one hundred health, social care and education professionals, and never once did any one of them ever in any way suggest any of us might be Autistic. I found me, then I found my children, and were that not to have been the case, we would have continued to remain lost. So, when I say the 'system' is incapable of finding us, this is why I say it, and I should add, our story is not an isolated one. I hear many similar accounts from late diagnosed Autistic people.

Laura, my eldest child, has experienced mental illness, comorbid physical health issues and challenges in many parts of her life. Today, she is happily married, and went on to have three more amazing children, my grandchildren, totalling a beautiful yet chaotic family of six! Laura works for my business and is an essential part of our team, which I will talk more about later in the book. Sadly, Laura will often say I am the *only* employer who would ever employ her given her own and her family's needs, and the flexibility she requires. I, on the other hand, think she goes the extra mile, gets the job done and that's all I require as an employer. How she gets to that point is flexible to meet her needs, she does it in her own way, not my way. Sadly though, I think Laura isn't wrong in her thinking. Employers have a long way to go in terms of flexibility and meeting the needs of Autistic people. Research shows only 22% of Autistics are in any kind of employment – full or part-time.[13] It's a sad statistic, though one I do also challenge on reliability…

Like all current Autism research, the employment research around Autism is based solely on those Autistics who are self-identified and/or diagnosed Autistic, not based on *all* Autistics, so we cannot truly *know* or say if only 22% of all Autistics are in any kind of employment, not until we find the rest. Until we know who *all* the Autistics are, what the 22% could really be telling us about is the impact of disclosure on our employment prospects. I predict that many of us *are* in fact in gainful full and part-time employment, and based on what I have now identified, many of us will be successful and at the *top of our game,* the latter being one of the very factors why we are yet to be found or will be the last to be found. Find us *all* and the 22% could look *very* different. This 'lost Autistic' blind spot exists across all Autism research and is yet another valuable reason why we need to find *all* Autistics. Until we do so, we cannot truly know Autism research is fully representative and therefore reliable.

Our family's journey highlights the hereditary nature of Autism. Not everyone is aware of the highly genetic nature of Autism. The condition is largely genetic, with some research also suggesting intrauterine exposure to chemicals being a potential cause, and the existence of acquired Autism, the latter brought about through changes in brain structure from damage or disease. Outside of this, we are looking at the aforementioned hereditary inheritance, which is proven to be up to 83%.[14] If a child is diagnosed Autistic, why are we *not* screening the parents for Autism, I ask? An expedient way of finding those who have been 'overlooked', is it not? This would, of course, require a mindset that views diagnosis as a treatment as much as a diagnostic undertaking, and sadly most people, including clinical professionals, are yet to fully comprehend the positive health benefits of diagnosis for so many Autistics, especially the late diagnosed ones.

Of course, not every Autistic experiences diagnosis positively, and not everyone wants to be assessed, or wants the Autism diagnosis and label, and therein lies one of the many ethical challenges of screening all biological parents. I believe if we can re-educate and conquer the pathologising and ableist attitudes and systems around Autism – ideas it is a bad thing – this barrier would dissolve naturally. Mostly, I come across Autistics who have found diagnosis positive and experienced better health outcomes as a result of being diagnosed, but I am mindful this isn't the case for everyone.

All too often, I find myself providing explanation to the question: "But what difference does a diagnosis make?" As someone who was lost and desperately searching for their identity for forty-five years, it is important, or it certainly was for me. It was *the* best psychological intervention I have *ever* received in my life, but one that I may not have needed if me and my Autistic ways had been accepted by society, and I hadn't internalised that I was broken and bad.

Given the strong genetic link in our family, our present and future family tree dwellers will need to be very alert and on the lookout for Autism where and when other suffering or challenges emerge. It could well be the explanation surrounding them. Our family is likely carrying a strong genetic code for neurodivergence, particularly Autism, but possibly ADHD also. As a side point, Autistics often connect well with other neurodivergent people, so in many cases we partner and marry our own neurotype or other neurodivergent people, rather than neurotypicals, and the rest is obvious, I would have thought. Again, I am not saying in *all* cases, but there are more than enough anecdotal examples to substantiate this (with a smidgen of blind spot and denial in some places, driven by lack of awareness, knowledge and ableism). I'm not sure about the empirical evidence for this 'pairing up', but I will quote Simon Baron-Cohen from his book *The Pattern Seekers*: "The absence of evidence, is not evidence of absence."[15]

In my memoir *The Umbrella Picker*, I talk about the pervasive sense I lived with for a very long time that I needed to 'break the cycle' of something in our family, but never quite knowing what it was that I was to provide cessation to. Today I recognise that it was to break the cycle of undiagnosed Autism in our family tree, and that I was to be the 'agent of change'. I found myself and my Autistic children, and because of this, generations of our family from here on in will never be missed or overlooked like the generations preceding us. Our stories and my books will create a legacy that will ensure Autism insight is available for future generations of my family, a privilege that my ancestors were not afforded and died without knowing. It saddens me that my grandmother and my great-grandmother likely died wondering what was wrong with them, when they just needed to know they were 'different' and that they were *amazing* because of that difference. If they were only here now…

Given this fact, and our family's newfound alertness to the traits of neurodivergence, in particular Autism, we have identified that two, possibly four out of four of my biological grandchildren are neurodivergent, with three of the four showing the signs of Autism. My two biological children who are diagnosed Autistic have different fathers, and my husband is not the biological grandparent of my grandchildren. That takes a little processing, I appreciate. I am the common biological denominator. Only last month, one of my grandchildren underwent a dyslexia screening, only for her mum, my daughter, to be told by the assessor, "No, she does not have dyslexia, but I do believe she has ADHD." And so forth, we embark on another lengthy journey towards neurological truth.

> Note: As I write today, I am adding an amendment to the above. My granddaughter, Violet, the second youngest of my four grandchildren, was last Friday formally diagnosed Autistic, with sensory processing disorder, and with a recommendation for an ADHD assessment as soon as possible. No more missed people in our family; it stopped with me.

> Additional note: As I write this final note, it is now November 2023 and my eldest grandchild has now received a formal Autism diagnosis, and my daughter Laura has now been officially diagnosed with ADHD, alongside her earlier diagnosis of Autism.

My daughter is one of the most tenacious fighters and neurodivergence advocates. Week in, week out, she attends clinical appointments trying desperately to seek solutions to the related health challenges in herself and her children, and to seek the necessary assessments for neurodivergence. There are a whole range of challenges – sleep issues, incontinence issues, gastrointestinal problems, physical disabilities, behavioural challenges – and my daughter's greatest fear is that someone at some stage will accuse *her* of FII (fabricated or induced illness). These are just some of the many challenges SEN parents are faced with, and that only other SEN parents truly understand. It is now September 2023 and my eldest grandchild, who has struggled with the transition to high school, is currently at home, waiting to view a SEN school and hoping that a place will be made available for her. If this does not happen, the decision has been made by her mum to home educate her. The struggles are ongoing, and they are daily for SEN parents, and for SEN grandparents.

As I wrote this (prior to the Notes above), we were still pursuing assessments, then three years in the waiting for the additional Autism assessments that were required for two of my grandchildren, and my daughter Laura herself had been waiting since September 2021 for an ADHD assessment, as recommended in her Autism report in the same month of that year. Even though the UK NICE guidelines on Autism[16] state that assessments should take place no more than three months following referral, there are systemic failures in achieving this in the UK. This doesn't consider the additional barriers and gatekeepers parents will also face *before* the referral is even made.

As I currently write, there are three local authority areas in England that are no longer undertaking assessments unless specific criteria are met at point of referral, changes that prevent people being eligible in the first place. Discriminatory screening software is being used to triage need. Sadly, I can see a future where the offering is removed altogether and families will need to self-finance all assessments for neurodivergence, not unlike cosmetic surgery. I don't even need to say that the system is broken, but I will say it – the system of assessment and support for neurodivergent people and their families in the UK is totally and utterly shambolic and broken. This frustrates me daily. It simply adds more suffering to those who already have, and do, suffer. It adds insult to our injury. We are viewed as a burden, only acknowledged through deficit, not through the strengths we possess, which can be capitalised upon if we are diagnosed and supported effectively. At the very least, we should be *accepted*, and at the very best, we should be *appreciated* and valued for who we are. And we should not have to beg for such human rights.

I hope one day to write a story that has found us all, one where all Autistics are supported effectively, and where Autism is viewed as a variant not a fault, and where we are appreciated. I am not disabled by my Autism. I am disabled by my anxiety and gastrointestinal problems, most likely occurring because I live in a society built and engineered to support the predominant neurotype or neurotypical brain type, not my own. Neurotypicals are not pathologised, so why then do we pathologise the neurodivergent brain? "Maybe it's the neurotypicals who are weird?" asks Fern Brady in a recent episode of *The Last Leg*.[17] This made me smile, but I am also of a mindset that subscribes to the belief that no one brain type is superior to another, but rather we will be superior as a human race when we can live harmoniously and co-operatively together. That is true neurodiversity!

Each time I write, we move a little further along the pathway of awareness, acceptance and support. I hope I have enough time left to see a better future, but you can be sure of one thing… while I am here and functioning, I will not ever stop trying to help those who are suffering to find themselves, to give them a voice, and to know they are simply different, not wrong. What Autistic people face is not inevitable, it was socially constructed. It just needs deconstructing and rebuilding better, and Autistics need to be leading the way. Another reason to find us!

CHAPTER 4

A Variant Not a Fault!

Historically, Autism has been viewed as a disability, and disability seen as something of a burden to our society, to be pitied, stereotyped, patronised, invalidated, discriminated against and generally viewed as lesser or inferior. There are pervasive, outdated stereotypes and beliefs that Autism is a mental illness, that many of us are learning disabled, that we misbehaved at school, and when playing with our toy cars would line them up in orderly fashion. Firstly, I didn't play with toy cars! But I did have thirty+ Sindy and Barbie dolls, a loving obsession with 'Crystal Barbie', whose home I set up beautifully and curated with fine attention to detail, but who I then did not play with because I did not see the value or pleasure in the social interaction of the figures or the imaginative play. The setting up *was* the play. This was my equivalent of lining cars up in a row. I also recall as a teenager being told by friends that the toiletries in my bedroom were stacked and arranged perfectly, like a shelf in a high street chemist, many not even opened, and would reach their use by date before use. My bedroom was the safe unmasked version of me, they had not seen this before, and it was met with suspicion and curiosity.

The outdated male-orientated stereotypes of Autism derive, amongst other things, from the fact that our understanding of Autism has been built around research that was performed on and with Autistic boys, rather than girls, and as a consequence, the knowledge and understanding of Autism in girls is behind and lacking, missing the pink, so to speak. It is also the very reason we are more blind to Autism in women, and women continue to be overlooked.

That said, I do feel the world is 'woke' to this fact now, and that things are changing in a favourable direction. That, of course, could be misjudgement on my part because I am exposed to the 'noise' around Autism and Autism in girls much more than most might be – related literature, social media, TV documentaries and my continued personal and professional development in areas that expose me to Autism 'noise'. I consider myself both an ambassador for my people, and an advocate for their acceptance and support (and my own), so I move within circles where I can do this, which could mean my perception is somewhat biased. Whether change *is* in fact occurring I cannot be one hundred percent sure, though my gut tells me it is, and there are more than enough pattern indicators I derive from my clients that tell me it is – though whether that is at a pace which will ever achieve parity with the knowledge of Autism in boys and men is yet to be seen. Only through concerted efforts to redress the balance – funding for and commitment to research focused on Autistic women and girls, hearing female narratives, supporting females to have a platform to share their narratives, etc. – will that change. The same can be equally said of non-binary groups, where the research and voices are also missing. My own interest area is certainly that of women, girls and non-binary in respect of Autism. I am particularly curious about the conditions for searching (and self-identification), as in who searches for themselves, and who does not, and at what lengths a person will search? My interest group is the lost and unidentified autistic, more so than the found, though it may be through the found that we learn more about the lost, particularly if they were found late. When I refer to 'the lost', I am referring to those autistics who do not know they are autistic. When I refer to the found, I am referring to those who self-identified (found themselves) or were identified by professionals (found by others). For research purposes, the lost are a difficult to find – but not impossible to find – sample group, even after their death, as was illustrated by a recent study about possible undiagnosed Autism in people who died by suicide.[18]

If we can understand the conditions for how Autistics become 'found' – identified and/or diagnosed – then we have a better chance of finding the missing group and addressing the barriers preventing them being found. We also get the chance to learn how they have survived, their coping mechanisms. I have a number of theories of how one gets from 'lost' autistic to 'found' Autistic. One is that the likelihood, and how much someone will search for themselves, the missing piece (no reference to jigsaw puzzles and associated organisations being made here) will come down to:

1. IQ.
2. Extent of suffering, i.e., the number and severity of co-existing mental/physical health issues.
3. The level of social masking and/or how much someone *wants* to 'fit in'.

These, I believe, are the conditions for the extent to which someone will search. The less these are present, the less someone will feel the need to search for what is missing and why they feel lost. All three would make up number two of my three requisite conditions for self-identification referred to earlier (a searching or receptiveness to an explanation not yet known). To understand that, and of course to prove it empirically, is to move closer to finding more Autistic people, or empowering them to find themselves, and removing the gap in society and research that is the huge blind spot of unidentified Autism. Other factors could inhibit these too, e.g., use of substances, as these have an impact on brain performance. The greater the use, the weaker the conditions for self-identification, as number two would be inhibited and diminished.

One thing is assumed of us all at birth. It is unwritten and unspoken, unlike weight, sex and time of birth, but it is always assumed. We are all assumed neurotypical, to have a neurotypical brain type, until there is irrefutable proof otherwise. And even when there is, it can still be incredibly difficult to prove it and to be believed. Proof of neurodivergence is often through pathologising the person and their traits, not through strength markers. The assumption that we are all neurotypical, simply because it is the predominant neurotype, will be wrongly assumed and incorrect in up to 20% of us, which is a lot of wrong assumptions. I also think that figure is an underestimate of the reality.

Such errors are not so profound or present in any other area of diversity, ethnic, or otherwise, because most other areas of diversity are not so difficult to identify. For example, I identify my ethnicity by my skin colour, the ethnicity of my biological parents, grandparents, and great-grandparents, and while not *totally* infallible – I could, for example, be an albino person of colour, rather than the white, fair-haired person I think I am – my conclusion would likely be correct. Other features substantiate my conclusion further, my hair texture and facial features tell me I am not an albino person of colour, and that I am very likely to be accurate in identifying the ethnicity part of my diversity profile. As an aside, I imagine albino people of colour live with the same sense of *where do I belong* that I live with. Imagine if they are undiagnosed autistic too, two minority identities, and the unique narrative linked to being both. Who is sharing their story? Neurotype isn't so easy to identify, so it's vital to understand the process leading up to identification, in order to find *others* who aren't there yet. Any research would need to use the appropriate definitions and measures for each contributory, and of course the most efficacious methodologies.

So, you might be thinking, why is finding all the unidentified autistics so vitally important? There are lots of reasons, but my own top three are these:

1. **Life preservation from suicide (suicide prevention):** Autistics have a three times higher suicidality than neurotypicals, so we need to know who the Autistics are to fully understand the contributories to thoughts of suicide in Autistics and what moves Autistic people from thoughts of suicide to suicide behaviour, and the best suicide interventions for Autistics. If we know who they are, we can put safety aids in place, e.g., should all Autistics, or at least all Autistics who have ever experienced thoughts of suicide, have a safety plan in place? We also need to test the current training and intervention programmes and supports, and be sure they are *still* effective for Autistics, i.e., do they still work when the person in need is Autistic?
2. **Child protection and safeguarding:** Autism is associated with an almost threefold increased risk of coercive sexual victimisation,[19] something I unfortunately share in my own lived experience, and document in my memoir *The Umbrella Picker*. Knowing *who* the Autistic children (and adults) are, and that they carry a double vulnerability, one by nature of being a child – all children are classed as vulnerable – *and* by them being Autistic, we can then afford these children the

extra protection and support they need to be extra vigilant and alert to predators. Saving Autistics from predators and preventing abuses also reduces this as a contributory factor of suicide (number one).
3. **Identity:** Autism is an identity, not just a medical condition; we deserve to know who we are and *why* we are, not live like I did for forty-five years unknowing and desperately searching and seeking identity in any other area I could find in order to fill the gaping void I was experiencing. Note: not all identities sought by undiagnosed autistics will be positive or socially acceptable, such as overly investing in a career, or academia identity. Some will be gangs and the gang culture identity this provides, or online eating disorder groups that exacerbate the illness rather than support recovery, or self-harm communities that normalise self-harm and belonging to such an extent that it increases severity, frequency, or both, and could lead to an unintended death.

If I was to sum up all three: We need to find the unidentified autistics to **SAVE LIVES**. Reason enough, don't you think?

Another benefit of identifying Autistic people, outside of those which are more Autistic individual focused, include the benefit of having *all* Autistic people included in **research**. To have the fullest picture of Autism, not just a picture based on the lucky ones of us who got found or managed to find ourselves. As it stands at present, all Autism research is based on the diagnosed or self-identified, it does not include those who are yet unfound. Finding them could dramatically change what we know about Autism.

If someone had found me and diagnosed me Autistic in childhood, I could have benefited from all of the above, had the chance to understand my own relationship with suicidal thoughts, why I was abused, why I wanted to be a mum from about the age of thirteen (if I had been in a relationship earlier, it would have happened earlier), not spent years searching in every identity I could find for who I was, and I may have been a valuable source of information for research that did not know I existed. Maybe *I* would have performed some of that research! If I had been found in my twenties, maybe the research I now wish to undertake would already have been undertaken and now be serving a benefit to the Autistic community? The losses are wide. My diagnosis has helped with number 1) my own life preservation; I have a safety plan in place, and since diagnosis the thoughts are more diluted at times, and number 3) I now know who and why I am, I know my core identity, not an assumed me, and I can be part of future research if invited to be, and in fact have already volunteered for some. As for number 2), I can't turn back time, but I am so much more alert to predators of any kind than I used to be. I am vigilant.

The not knowing left me feeling I was 'faulty', my diagnosis told me I was just 'different' and that my difference was a variation, but never a 'fault'. What I have further come to understand in the last five months, and which forms the essence of this book, is that **my difference, the**

variation, was more than just 'not being faulty', it is the very thing that has determined my strengths, and what has *caused* me to be successful. It is not lesser, it is not equal to, it is better than that!

Autistic people will experience the world and behave differently to neurotypicals. From a clinical and social point of view, Autism is often viewed pathologically in negative ways. The DSM-5 manual defines Autism Spectrum Disorder (note: the use of disorder rather than difference) as "persistent difficulties with social communication and social interaction" and "restricted and repetitive patterns of behaviours, activities or interests" (this includes sensory behaviour), present since early childhood, to the extent that these "limit and impair everyday functioning."[20] We are not referring to 'a little bit' Autistic. This does not exist, you either are, or you are not. If we were all 'a little bit Autistic', it would simply be a part of the human condition, like having eyes. Those diagnosed must meet the specific criteria and to a specified level. The latter denotes the fact that those who are not suffering or impaired in any way, to a sufficient clinical level, would not meet criteria for diagnosis and therefore *not* be Autistic, so it's not just sufficient to have Autistic traits, it's about impact on everyday functioning as well. This being the case, it's possible there are people with Autistic traits, but who would not clinically be judged as Autistic. Is it possible to have all the traits, and *not* experience the negative impacts that surround them, I wonder? Right now, my brain is thinking unlikely, maybe more a lack of awareness or denial in the person? This is yet another answer it would be useful to know and understand. When Autistic traits exist but there are no difficulties, why is that? What does that person have in their defence?

The pathologising of Autism, like many things, is a social construction, and one of the factors that contributes to our negative experiences. What if instead the world suddenly respected and valued Autistic traits and profiles, said this is how everyone should be and act, and if they can't, we will treat them negatively, so *they* will feel 'othered' and are forced to mask out their neurotypical traits to be Autistic? We would force neurotypicals to keep to restricted and predicted ways of doing things, suppress the fact that they wanted more variety and change, and make them feel they must communicate directly and to the point, no need for any social pleasantries. Small talk would be frowned upon as a pointless and needless waste of time, those who partook in it rejected, and the other myriad of traits and presentations visible in neurotypicals would be seen as faulty and wrong, rather than different. Oh, and if the neurotypicals failed to 'mask out' their neurotypical traits successfully, we would label them as 'weird', distance ourselves from them, and they may even find themselves party to disciplinary procedures if they were lucky enough to be in gainful employment, or criminalised if their associated neurotypical behaviours were misunderstood in the wrong place at the wrong time. Because the reverse of this exists, I can think of so many occasions when I have not felt listened to in a group, overpowered by the talkers in a workplace meeting, not had the neurotypical social skills to assert myself, and just reached the point of learned helplessness – I just stopped speaking and fully disengaged.

> Note: lack of understanding in the workplace and in the criminal justice system can and does expose many Autistics to punitive practices and disciplinary procedures for being themselves, again because what is an acceptable workplace behaviour or societal conduct is constructed for neurotypicals not for neurodivergents who are Autistic or otherwise neurodivergent, so even if we are a highly intellectual individual, our social intelligence is perceived as below par, and our low social intelligence gets us into trouble.

One in four of our prison population is believed to have ADHD.[21] One in four! How well, I wonder, would neurotypicals adapt to fit into *our* world if we were the majority neurotype? Do we only pathologise Autism, and other neurodivergent conditions such as ADHD, because they exist as minorities – are we simply *not* the loud enough voice rather than because of what these conditions *actually* are? Is Autism only pathologised because of who is doing the pathologising, and the fact that we are small in number?

What is acceptable in our society is a social 'gold standard' created by and for neurotypicals. If the minority neurotype had created what is acceptable, *their* socially constructed version, it would suit us the minority perfectly well, but may not then suit the current majority. How much we are disabled by the condition itself is debatable and each Autistic person will have their own views based on their experiences. The questions might instead be, is it a **disability**? A **difference**? Or even a **disorder**? Context will often dictate this, and for me, the case I can create for each can sometimes make me feel like my thinking is flaky and changeable.

DSM-5 the diagnostic and statistical manual titles Autism a *disorder*, worthy of diagnosis in its manual. I received a *diagnosis* of Autism spectrum *condition* in my assessment report, not *disorder*. Disorder wording was not used. Whether we get into the semantics of disorder or condition, either can only be assigned to me by someone qualified to do so, and who understands the Autism diagnostic process *sufficiently* to do so effectively. For what it is worth, I prefer to use the word **condition**. I am *different* not disordered; this I always knew, which was the very reason I was searching for my 'why' in the first place, but I also believe I am *disabled*, though not by the Autism itself. I am disabled by the co-existing/comorbid illnesses that seem to be connected to my being Autistic, whether caused by living in a society that does not accept my 'difference' or another cause, which is linked to the Autism.

> Note: the UK Government's Equality Act 2010 defines a disability as 'a physical or mental impairment that has a 'substantial' and 'long-term' negative effect on your ability to do normal daily activities, of which

STRENGTH *not* DEFECIT

each element has been interpreted through the body of case law that has come of this since its inception in 2010'.[22]

My anxiety and gastric problems never ever go away, they are long-term, but it's clear that they started the moment I was exposed to other people at nursery school in addition to my primary caregiver (my mum) at the age of three. They didn't feature in my first memory on the wooden playframe, and I don't have memories that pre-date eighteen months of age. I constantly live with managed anxiety and managed gastrointestinal problems, and they most definitely *do* have an impact on me every single day, doing normal daily activities. For example, talking to other human beings, and my need to access bathrooms, the frequency of this, the accompanying stomach pains, and intense fear and panic. Therefore, according to the Equality Act 2010, and the UK Government who created it, what I am is **disabled**. Interestingly, I am not classified as **disabled** by the same UK Government's Department for Work & Pension's Personal Independence Payment (PIP) assessment process, so I am not eligible for financial support for the disability they say I have by way of their definition, despite the costly 'Autism tax' I pay daily to accommodate the **disabilities** I have that meet *their* criteria under *their* Equality Act 2010. For example, needing to take a cab instead of the Tube when I deliver my training courses in London so that I can manage and cope with the stress and overwhelm in order to still deliver my training effectively, and absorbing that cost rather than passing it on to my client. As I highlighted at the outset, context matters, and it's changeable. And the decision and assigning of labels is not always going to be mine to make!

In my case, the permanent levels of anxiety, and permanent gastric problems, are what disable me. The question becomes, if I was accepted and supported by neurotypicals in the ways that I needed, would these comorbids go away? Do they exist simply because I live in a society that does not really understand, accept and support Autistics, and if this was to change, *would* they go away? I'm not sure that I will ever get the opportunity to find that out, but I am still hopeful. Even if I was fully accepted and supported, I'm not one hundred percent sure that they would go away, and I'd never be able to account for the forty-eight years of damage already predetermined – it would require a blank slate from the start – but I *can* tell you that my anxiety spikes around any interaction with human beings, and to this day it remains the case that 'people' are what scare me above all else in life, and I think this is what triggers the physical gastric reaction I have. I am in and out of fight or flight all the time, and I stay in the state longer than would be the case for someone with 'normal' anxiety, the anxiety that is a natural part of the human condition. I am most definitely disabled by the comorbids, but I'm not sure they would totally go away in any change of circumstance. Therefore, I do see my Autism as both a *difference* and a *disability*, and clinically, a *condition*, but for me, not a *disorder*.

STRENGTH *not* DEFECIT

To understand Autism is to understand what each means, but more importantly what they mean for each Autistic person. I only speak for me. If I speak for others, I silence their voice, and their voice deserves to be heard as much as my own does. Ask *them*, then do them the service of listening. In my work in mental health, and when supporting Autistic people, I always advocate for the 'person-centred' approach. We should always ask and never assume in any case. Asking can help us to meet a person's preferences, but it also communicates 'you matter, and I care', and that can sometimes be even more helpful than meeting the actual need, especially for people who for a long time may have felt like they didn't, and that no one cares. Unfortunately, it still permeates my own thinking.

The intention of my last book *The Umbrella Picker* was to help find other 'lost girls', those who are still suffering, by illustrating the female presentation of Autism so that they could 'connect' the right information at the right time. The purpose of this book is to make a case for our strengths over our deficits, to highlight that it was our very strengths that kept many of us hidden for so long, because we will be the highest of high achievers past and present – both in our professional fields, where we will often be the top of our game, socially competent and perhaps hyperlexic in our speech (wide and enhanced vocabulary from a very young age) and show successes in our personal lives (in my case long-distance running, including marathons, twelve half marathons, and more 10k runs than I can even recall). If we are business owners, we will often be successful business owners. I also aim to highlight the two key Autistic drivers that created this, drivers that neurotypicals might benefit from knowing, and most importantly, to remove and reduce the ableism that is currently preventing people in this group from being found. There is potentially a very large quantity of people in this group who do not know they are autistic, hidden by their success and the ableism and disablism that discriminates against disabled people, but also has an impact on those not recognised as disabled, in this case, the unfound unidentified autistic. Ableism can be defined as:

> *… A set of beliefs or practices that devalue and discriminate against people with physical, intellectual, or psychiatric disabilities and often rests on the assumption that disabled people need to be 'fixed' in one form or the other.*
> Centre for Disability, 2023 [online][23]

Autistic profiles like that described above and my own are possibly *the* most hidden and hardest to reach of all unidentified autistics – the last to be found. My own profile will, I hope, challenge the outdated stereotypes of Autistic presentation. Our being missed will be *precisely* **BECAUSE** we were and are successful. Being missed is also based on a mistaken belief that suffering and capability are mutually exclusive, that they cannot exist together, and yet they so often do – bedfellows even. Support should not be conditional on the absence or presence of capability or success. We overcame the odds (or deficits) that would have found us when you view us through an ableist lens.

The unidentified autistic person themselves will by no means be immune to the influence of this ableism. Along with those around them, they too will unlikely be entertaining any idea that they may be autistic because of Autism still being associated with low achievement and capability, and *not* being seen as synonymous with high ability and high achievement. Unless the Autistic is savant Autistic – who are very small in number in the Autistic community, a double minority, who might often have other high support needs (considered the disability) that have led to them being identified earlier, despite their apparent 'superpower' of excellence in a particular area – their autism is unlikely to be identified. The unidentified autistics I am referring to are those who present as all-round high achievers who are hiding in plain sight, but who still suffer incredibly.

Only today I read a quote from another late diagnosed Autistic, Dr Mary Doherty, a Consultant Anaesthetist, about her own late diagnosis: "The possibility of being autistic never entered my head. I had a very stereotypical view of autism, and I certainly did not fit that." No connection is being made between their abilities and these being linked to them being Autistic, or the possibility that success might even mirror Autistic traits. Autism is too often viewed through a lens of deficiency, particularly social deficiency, savant-ist thinking and ableist attitudes, and high social masking *successful* Autistics will simply not be on the radar, other than the radar of other self-identified and/or diagnosed Autistics, who often have a fine-tuned neuroscope and the ability to spot other Autistics in their presence, perhaps in some cases another illustration of their exceptional pattern-seeking abilities, and heightened sensory perceptions.

We are often skilled at spotting fellow Autistics, though again, only clinical judgement can confirm or deny the actual presence of Autism because of the way things are done at the moment. Until the stereotypes are fully challenged and our thinking changes, we will always miss the highest achieving Autistics, and they will be reliant only on themselves to self-identify, which may never happen, as would have been the case for me was the right information not put right in front of me at the right time, in our case because we happened by chance to be exploring our son's challenging behaviour. Today I feel ashamed that we referred to it as 'challenging behaviour', but it was illustrative of our own ableist views at the time. Oliver's behaviour is normal for an Autistic but seen as challenging if viewed through a neurotypical lens. Sometimes I still need to remind myself which lens I should be using! Because of how blind I was prior to my own self-identification, my first book *The Umbrella Picker* was quite genuinely the book I wish someone had written for me decades earlier. It would have saved years of untold searching and suffering, plus that of my children.

The missing of Autistic people is a tragedy of our past, which needlessly continues in the present, but it is not inevitable. In most cases we *will* be suffering, there will be past or present evidence of this somewhere – a mental 'breakdown', copious amounts of alcohol consumed to

STRENGTH *not* DEFECIT

cope with life, over-working, issues with sleep, and/or disordered eating. Since some of this is socially accepted and present in many Allistics (non-Autistics) as well, it is unlikely to be questioned by themselves or those around them, in relation to unidentified Autism. Unidentified autistics can also be blinded by the unspoken thinking that everyone is experiencing what they are experiencing – after all, we only know our own experiences – they don't yet know otherwise – that they too are 'different' – so they dismiss it, or they de-validate it.

The signs of suffering may be much more of a hidden kind, or perhaps a behaviour that is socially accepted in the circles in which they move. Imagine the financier who is top of their game, and who frequently socialises after work with fine food and drink, and who is not cataloguing the volume of alcohol consumed that has become a standard part of their coping because it is a socially accepted thing to do in their sector, a social lubricant, maybe even the running joke on birthdays and celebrated with alcohol-themed birthday cards and gifts. In my own younger years, I too would use alcohol to cope with socially demanding situations, nights out with friends, and particularly at work get-togethers, which others would relish and I hated but partook in to 'fit in'. Fortunately, in the industries I had worked, they were very infrequent, but what if they hadn't been? What if to be 'good at my job' required me to drink and party as hard as I worked? I recall a human resources worker years ago celebratorily saying, "…and you know, they party as hard as they work," about a lawyer. She was endorsing it, it was totally socially acceptable, the inference being, if they didn't, they would somehow have been lesser. I have always strived to be good at my job (conscientious, and worked incredibly hard), and so too I would have strived to be 'good' at the social too, which would for me (and others like me) have created a dangerous risk were that the requirement. These are just some of the unidentified autistic people who might benefit from the connection being made and from being found. Again, ableist views operate as a barrier.

Autism might not fit with someone's ideas of perfection, and many Autistics, particularly undiagnosed autistic women, are perfectionists, so you see how some would reject the idea, even when the information is right in front of them. That was the pre-diagnosis me, too, perfectionist. My achievements pre-diagnosis were all too often about impressing others and trying desperately to feel good about myself. Today my ambitions are not driven by perfection, they are driven by healthy intention, which is very different, though to others they may still be seen as perfectionism (I cannot control that). Why didn't my perfectionism get in the way of me self-identifying my Autism? Why didn't it prevent number two in my three criteria for self-identification being realised, Autism not fitting with my ideas of 'perfection'? The reason is because my desperation to find the truth, the searching, far outweighed any ableism present in me at the time. I needed my answer to 'why' so much more than my need to be viewed as 'perfect'. Furthermore, I didn't truly see

Autism as imperfection – the ableism wasn't so dominant in me, so I didn't view an Autism diagnosis as damaging. If anything, it has done the opposite, it has aided my business and career immensely, and I had the foresight to know it would. It has offered a valuable dynamic and knowledge to my work in mental health. The greatest challenge I have at the moment is that my growing knowledge and understanding of Autism is ahead of the evidence base in mental health, so I have to censor myself. But it's not possible to unknow what you know, just because others are not yet up to speed on it, especially when you are Autistic – we pride facts and honesty.

My work helps me to illustrate to others what Autistics can and do achieve. I am able to challenge any stereotyped ideas and show learners their blind spot. Because until I disclose that I am Autistic, most people don't think they have this blind spot. The blind spot is that they think they know what an Autistic looks like, and I am not *it*. But I am. My disclosure shows them what they don't know, it challenges any presence of ableism. It's an interesting observation when I share my late diagnosed Autistic lived experience, the shift in demeanour, looking for an explanation that isn't ableist. They:

- Eye me curiously, searching for the deficit. What did they miss beforehand? Where is the chink in my armour? There *must* be one.
- Or they infer it's wrong, I must be wrong, or maybe the person who assessed me got it wrong, the fallibility

on my side not theirs due to the now likelier deficit in me than them.
- Or they *do* acknowledge it, with the caveat… maybe she's just not *very* Autistic or she must be one of those 'high-functioning' ones.

Anything other than the possibility that my strengths exist *BECAUSE* I am Autistic, or the more inconvenient truth, that *their* views are ableist.

Once you know you have a blind spot, you then (hopefully) question how many others you aren't aware of, which opens up a whole world of possibility. This book, I am sure, will reveal my own blind spots to some readers. I know I have them, just not what they are. I don't know what they are because they are just that – blind spots – but I am always willing to learn, and that is all I can ask of others, just a willingness to learn. No blame.

Despite the barriers, I am in fact yet to come face-to-face with a late diagnosed Autistic who hasn't suffered for not being found in some way, and who hasn't experienced benefit in their late diagnosis, even if it *has* been difficult to process. That said, someone recently commented on a social media post that there is not enough talk of the diagnosis being a curse. Is Autism a curse? Or is the curse how society treats Autistic people, those of us identified or diagnosed Autistic who choose to disclose, or how society treats people who it recognises as 'different'? Is the curse more the negative experiences those people have encountered and internalised from society which have contributed to their own self-stigma and a belief that Autism is a curse? Nevertheless, the comment and use of the word 'curse' reminds me just how much Autistic people have and do suffer. In respect of labels, much like an Autism assessment can result in a label of Autistic, there are plenty of psychological screening tools that can offer labels and explanations of human thinking and behaviour, for example, Myers-Briggs type indicator, etc. We are often curiously interested in *these* findings, but they are not stigmatised by society. I'm yet to hear someone say to me how discriminated they've been because they are an ENTP or an ISFJ Myers-Briggs type, or how their type is a curse! The only difference is that one is pathologised and stigmatised, the others not. As an aside, some do believe the INFJ type to be very closely profiled with Autism. I happen to be an INFJ but have never been treated negatively because of that fact. Why then can't we be equally curious or interested in our neurotype without pathology? The diagnosis or label isn't the curse. It is living in a society that does not support, accept, or appreciate the Autistic neurotype and those with it... and in many cases, how much we have internalised the shame of that narrative.

The added benefit of establishing who has an Autistic neurotype is establishing what strengths the Autistic neurotype brings to the neurodiversity party – many still missing from this picture didn't get their invite! We may learn that success does in fact mirror Autism, or Autism mirrors success, and then the whole of neurodiversity can capitalise and benefit from this understanding too. No one neurotype is superior to another, and no neurotype is greater than the sum of its parts, but to understand each allows us all to benefit.

I am in no doubt that any success in life that I have achieved *largely* lies in the fact that I am Autistic, and I have now made the mental connections to which parts of my Autism have driven that success. But wouldn't it be useful to know if what I have established is the same for other Autistics who were, or are, hidden?

Now that I've established the connections between my own Autism and my successes, I can share them with others so they can explore any potential benefit for themselves. Learning from Autistic elders could be so valuable. I am living proof that there doesn't have to be limits when Autism is present, quite the opposite, in fact. I do, of course, fully appreciate that yes there are Autistics who will have significant support needs and care requirements, but what I am illustrating here is that there are other Autistics who don't fit the stereotype and whose voices have not been heard, and whose experiences have not been represented. I have also come across cases of Autistics with very high support needs, and who show excellence in a particular area. I recently watched a thirteen-year-old girl on TV who was blind, non-verbal and Autistic, who left audiences speechless when she played a highly complex Chopin piece in front of strangers at Leeds train station. Her high support needs were clear and obvious as she walked up to the piano with help, at which point the minds of the audience, while having a good idea what she was about to do, were being dissuaded by ableism (not fully acknowledging its presence, but I sense liking the challenge to it nevertheless). She too is living proof of what can be achieved, and that we should not be fooled by ableism.[24] I saw the same two factors, which I believe are fundamental to success, present in Lucy's success, illustrated by the background story her mum presented on her behalf, as I see in my own success. The only difference is that expectations of Lucy would be far less than of me because my challenges aren't so obvious to other people, and my support needs are not so great, unless I am suicidal. This can change everything. But she too proved people wrong. She was amazing, and without the support needs in other areas, could easily have been an autistic who slipped through the net due to her excellence. She might instead have been hidden in plain sight playing in a world-famous orchestra. Maybe the bigger question is, why isn't she?

The unfound are the autistics we know even less about, the people we have so much to learn from. Because we were missed, there is a huge gap in knowledge here, and who better to illustrate some of what that is than those of us who fit that very profile. We are far more likely to see our strengths than just seeing the deficits, as many of us won't have known we had limitations because we didn't know we were autistic and therefore hadn't internalised any idea we were incapable or 'disabled'. Maybe the thirteen-year-old girl hadn't internalised limitations either, maybe she just did what she was passionate about. Not knowing you are autistic, or not getting labelled 'disabled', means we don't see the barriers, or we just worked harder to overcome them, sometimes smashing the barriers into obliteration. I see this as one of only a few positives of late diagnosis – no one told us we couldn't, we didn't internalise we couldn't, and so we just *did* – but it only exists because of ableism. Expanding what we know and positively affirming Autism through a neuro-affirming narrative is key to positive change.

I am asking you to consider with an open mind as I proceed to illustrate how my own Autism has created what I have achieved in my lifetime. We must, however, keep in mind that each Autistic will have their own view of how much challenge, deficit, or indeed strength, exists for them. They set their limits, not others for them, including me. Any definition of 'success' is also of question here. Given that I was undiagnosed autistic for forty-five years, and that I have internalised common neurotypical ideals of success, it is these that I am referring to and will use as part of my illustration. My view of what success is today has in fact shifted, increasing more towards creating positive change for Autistic people, well-being, contentment, minimalism, spirituality, but I am appealing here to various associations of success.

CHAPTER 5

Obsess about It, and You'll be Successful at It!

Those of you who have read my memoir *The Umbrella Picker* will already know my thoughts on the language around Autism, and that I refer to my Autistic obsessions as just that – obsessions – rather than referring to them as special interests, or SPINS, as so many Autistics do. When I think of a 'special interest', I think it sounds like having a keen interest in a hobby, which doesn't even come close to the level at which I will invest myself in my obsessions, so I just keep it true to fact in terms of my own experience, though I am aware others prefer to use the term 'special interest' and I respect their choice to do so. Switch it in your mind as you read if you find it helpful to do so.

Invest might sound like my obsessions are a bit of a toll, but they are most definitely not. Unlike obsessions referred to in mental illnesses such as obsessive compulsive disorder (OCD), we are instead talking about the kind of obsession that makes us happy. Due to having hyperconnected brains, Autistics tend to feel passionate about the things they love – obsessions – so when we have

OBSESS ABOUT IT, AND YOU'LL BE SUCCESSFUL AT IT!

one, we overly fixate on it. Many, but not all Autistic people will have special interests/obsessions, and of those that do, they will enjoy them, immensely. We rarely must stop an obsession, they simply phase out when they are done with, and others might develop instead. We can also have multiple obsessions at any one time. The number of and type of obsession an Autistic person has, and whether they are socially acceptable obsessions, will also influence how successful they become or how successful the person is perceived to be. Some obsessions become and will remain lifetime obsessions, others just temporary. Autism itself, and everything that goes with it, has become one of my own obsessions, and I am pretty sure it will be one that will remain for the rest of my living days. Had I known I was Autistic earlier, it would have commenced earlier.

My late brother, who was also Autistic, had a lifetime obsession and fascination with buses. He was a self-professed 'bus fanatic'. His dream? To become a bus driver, of course! Unfortunately, Robert was told by many professionals – clinical psychologists, psychiatrists and other 'naysayers' – that his learning disability, mental illness and Autism would prevent him from realising his dream, and it would be unlikely he would ever work full-time, nor would he become a bus driver.

Incorrect in this assertion and caused by what Cohen[25] describes as 'clinician's illusion' – biases around recovery and ability due to clinicians' dominant exposure to those who are unwell rather than those who are well, leading to inaccurate beliefs about recovery and ability – they were proven wrong. In Robert's case, this showed itself as: these people with Autism, mental illness *and* learning disability are unable to perform this or similar tasks, therefore Robert (with Autism, mental illness and learning disability) will not be able to either. They totally underestimated the power of Autistic obsession!

Robert went on to prove them all wrong, not to prove them wrong per se (he wasn't ego driven), but simply because his dream was also his Autistic obsession. From a young age, Robert was obsessed with buses, but also obsessed with driving. He passed his car driving test at seventeen in just four weeks. At twenty-one, in 1997, without a learning disability, it took me well over a year to learn to drive and to pass my test. It was not my obsession in the slightest, and I continued with the lessons because of pressure from someone else to do so.

> Note: it's an oversight to ever underestimate an Autistic whose dream or career is fuelled by Autistic obsession, or if they have made an obsession out of their career. They simply find resources and ways around the barriers and anything that is disabling the dream, whether that is factors related to the Autism, another disability, or people.

I am curious as to how much this type of ableism is adding to the missing of Autistic people by clinical professionals, missing people who are all-round high achievers like me? What it does to one group, it also does in reverse to another, its manifestation just a different type of negative outcome, but still ableist.

One year prior to my brother's passing from terminal bowel cancer at forty-one, he proved them *all* wrong. Robert qualified as a bus driver, sought gainful employment with a South Yorkshire bus company, and was thriving. Sadly, the cancer which was also developing during this time took away the dream and his life. We miss him incredibly. My parents will never come to terms with the loss, especially my mother, who is now herself self-identified autistic, and is experiencing a lot of challenges moving forward from the pain and loss. Many neurotypical people fail to understand the extent of her grief, which she does not mask, and which is totally all-consuming and of itself obsessive, the nature and extent of which I will come on to in the next chapter.

Again, you will see here the hereditary nature of the Autistic condition, in my brother also being Autistic, and my mum, though it was rarely talked about in our family. Instead, all focus was on Robert's learning disability, which likely sidetracked everyone from increased understanding of Autism, and earlier diagnosis in myself, my mum, and my children. This is my brother's story produced prior to my own Autism self-identification and diagnosis https://youtu.be/HrsfkBTWj74 from my company's website. You will see no reference to Autism, only to Robert's learning disability.

I've had many an obsession over the years, some are short-term, some have greater longevity. Early childhood ones included, for a short time, horses, select toys, making clothes and a whole array of 'collections'. I was obsessed with ballet shoes, totally obsessed with wanting long hair and obsessed with the number five – this one does still exist. It started with the number four, and it moved on to the number five and stayed there. This statement is, I feel, so stereotypically Autistic. I can't even explain why, but it is. It is loaded with overstated logic, I guess.

I have developed people obsessions, real life people who I know or knew, and famous people who I do not know. I only have one person obsession now (which is slowly phasing out), a deceased famous person. My current obsessions are as follows:

- People (lifetime fascination and interest).
- Blind spots, i.e., the bit we miss in anything (started July 2023).
- Running (since late 2020).
- Reading and books (since as long as I could read, aged three).
- Mental health and mental illness, anything mind related (since 1998).
- My company, Mind Matters www.mindmatterstraining.co.uk (since 2015).
- My jobs since leaving school, with the exception of two – both of which I left within six months and where no obsession formed. There have been five, plus two businesses, one of which is Mind Matters – all obsessions.
- Autism (since the day I self-identified in 2020).
- Writing my book(s) – I'm at my most happy and fulfilled right now, doing this!

- My home and garden (we moved house in 2022, so curating my 'safe' space and my garden to my own idea of perfection is quite obsessive).

My obsessions don't have to be fuelled, nor do they have to be ended. An obsession ends itself; I do not choose it. I just slowly become less fulfilled by it; it stops giving me the dopamine hit that it might have done previously. There is no mourning for my obsessions, either. I don't look back on past ones with sadness or loss, they just make me happy at the time, and collectively have enriched my existence, perhaps even allowed my existence, as I am not sure that I would have survived without them. To say they are my life blood would not be an overstatement. Past ones include:

- Travel.
- Home décor projects.
- Arts and crafts projects.
- Underwater world and scuba diving.
- So very nearly – electric pylons!

Now, I have to say, the scuba diving one *is* one of my few obsessions that seriously did need to be ended, as it was indeed a threat to my existence. If I had known then what I know today, I would have ended it sooner. I did not know my limits because I didn't think I had any, but I did have some, and scuba diving was most definitely outside of my limits and capability. I experience anxiety, and in some situations, I panic and have meltdowns or close downs where I go non-verbal. I can flip from high to low-functioning in less than the time it takes you to make a cup of tea, and since I do both, I do not identify with either label. Instead, I say, "I am neither, yet I am both."

Like all scuba divers, I had to be medically 'signed off' and approved 'fit to scuba dive' by my GP, who when I asked, "Will my anxiety be an issue?" answered, "It's okay, anxiety is not a mental illness anyway." Don't even get me started on how he could have asserted that when I had an ongoing diagnosis of generalised anxiety disorder on my medical records at that point. Clearly, I wasn't referring to the everyday anxiety we all experience, otherwise there would be no scuba divers at all, because we all experience that kind of anxiety from time to time. I was referring to my clinical diagnosis of an *anxiety disorder.*

In 2014, we were in Mexico and chose to do one of our advanced diving qualifications while on holiday. To pass, we had to do various diving activities including a deep dive (60-100ft), drift dive, navigation and compass skills, amongst others. My husband and I both passed. For those of you who have been to Mexico, you may well have seen or heard about the Cenotes – ancient sinkholes in the Yucatan Peninsula – creating underground caverns, which many divers want to explore. They are on most divers' bucket list, but not for the fainthearted, and most certainly not for the claustrophobic! My husband and I were both planning to dive the Cenotes, but something told me I wasn't 'fit' for it, it wasn't going to be *right* for me, my 'gut feeling' was shouting to be heard. I decided my husband should go solo with the diving team. To this day, I am not sure I would have surfaced from the underground caverns alive. You cannot simply rise to the top, there isn't a top, or at least the top is not light and oxygen rich (or if it is, not for very long). I don't even want to describe it; it makes me feel sick and headachy just thinking about it right now. It's definitely triggering for me to write this. I tell myself I am safe in order to calm myself. I am very visual and when I am thinking about something like this I may as well be there as if it is really happening. Each time I read this section back, I am there, the panic starts to rise, I want to cry. Being visual is fantastic when the visions are positive – dreams and intentions – but it's a curse when they are not. One of my favourite quotes is a Henry Ford quote, which sums up perfectly the outcome of positive or negative vision, especially in relation to self-belief and achievement:

> *'Whether you think you can, or whether you think you can't – you're right.'*
>
> Henry Ford

What I think, I visualise – in detail… and what I visualise often materialises!

I've become proficient in compartmentalising the bad stuff as much as possible. The diving thankfully became an obsession of the past. My husband and I spoke about the diving and the Cenotes trip recently and today we both agree that neither of us would go back to this hobby (or as it was for me, this obsession). Diving was a beautiful experience at the time, it was the visuals that attracted me to it. The beauty of the undersea world is absolutely phenomenal and allowed me to switch off from the world above that I don't find easy to live in. When relaxed, it gave me an alternative world. We have dived with the manta rays at the cleaning stations in the Maldives, have some beautiful photos, and my husband has dived with nursing sharks, but we have both 'peaked' and are happy at that. The reality is I was never actually obsessed with the scuba diving itself, I was obsessed with the underwater world, and scuba diving was the only financially accessible conduit to fully immersing myself into it. Living in the UK, it is also quite difficult for a scuba obsession to manifest; the conditions are less likely (but not impossible) to come together, e.g., opportunities to practise scuba, and therefore I was unable to become successful at it in the way that I could my other obsessions. It didn't have the hallmarks of obsession.

> Note: My successes exist purely because they were/are driven by Autistic obsession, and I only become highly successful at them if they become an obsession.

I am fascinated and obsessed with tropical fish, not the cold-water underworld that exists in the UK, and I am *not* obsessed with the process of scuba, the equipment, or the diving community, etc. What fascinates me is the colour and the beauty of the tropical underworld, it is *mesmerising*!

If I had known then that I was Autistic and need to be

OBSESS ABOUT IT, AND YOU'LL BE SUCCESSFUL AT IT!

obsessed about something to be successful at it, I wouldn't have contemplated most of those dives. I am better able to protect my health and manage my safety risk by knowing and having an awareness that I *do* have 'limits' and that these link intrinsically to my obsessions, although I clearly had enough awareness back then, otherwise I would have done the dive… and may not have lived to tell the tale. It is important to say that scuba diving is not simply a 'no go' for Autistics, it's just understanding each spiky Autistic profile and knowing whether it is right for a particular Autistic person. My Autistic challenge was the cognitive overload associated with scuba equipment and instructions. There were too many practical tasks to manage, and when I am highly anxious, my brain doesn't work so well, and I am unable to make decisions quickly. My poor working memory also makes it difficult to remember lists of instructions if not written down. The consequence of not being able to do these things underwater is absolute.

It can be quite difficult for others to understand our obsessions, and sometimes, I will hide my own from certain people, mask them out, play them down. I do this because others don't truly understand them, or my need to do them over and above other things, and I pick up on negative cues that tell me this – smirks, joking comments, glazed eyes, boredom, distraction, questions said with a tone of judgement, people telling me they've had enough of it, etc. Many Autistics express that they feel misunderstood, and this is just one area of misunderstanding. The misunderstanding itself isn't the issue for me, it's the unwillingness of others to *try* to understand, and the pressure I've internalised to *always* be the one to adapt. One thing I cannot adapt, under any circumstance, however, is my need to 'do' my obsessions. If they are not accepted, they don't stop, I just hide them. They are like a driving urge, something I look forward to, an itch that always needs scratching, and they satisfy. Even the looking forward to spending time on my obsessions is a great feeling. If I am not 'doing' my obsessions, I am thinking about them, or looking forward to partaking in them. Obsessive-thinking about obsessions might even be described as one of them in and of itself.

Let me give you an idea of where I place my obsessions in the grand scheme of things. Think Maslow's Hierarchy of Needs, as illustrated in this image.

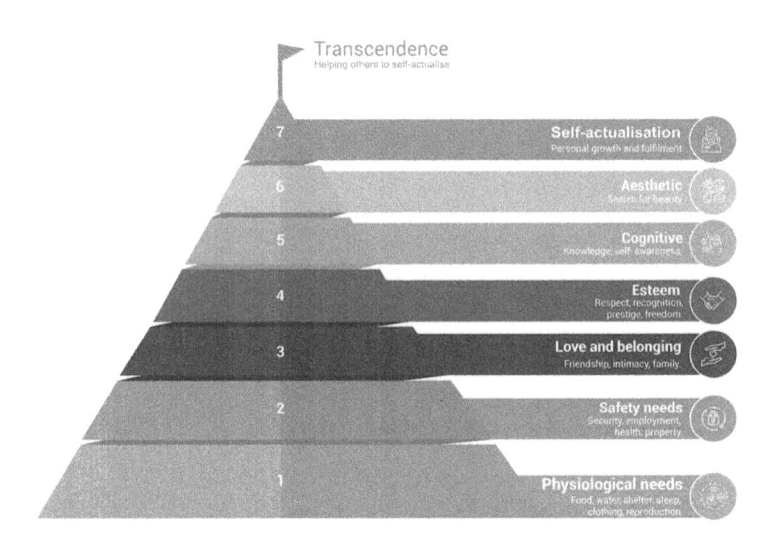

OBSESS ABOUT IT, AND YOU'LL BE SUCCESSFUL AT IT!

We are all working up the pyramid in the hope of reaching a place where we self-actualise – living creatively and realising our full potential – or further still reaching a place of 'transcendence'. Physiological needs are situated at the bottom. Here we are referring to food, water, warmth, rest, basic needs, if you will. We then move up to safety, physical and psychological safety, and security needs. Pretty much after that is where Autistic obsession comes in for me, before anything else. Some might even say Autistic obsessions are situated even further down, with physiological or below. I would even concede that my own might be. I have already highlighted my obsessions have been fundamental to my existence, just like food and water, for example. In fact, sometimes, I will neglect my *other* basic needs when I am in full flow obsession, hyper and monotropic focused. As I write now, I am asking myself, have I eaten or drunk enough? Am I bursting to go to the loo? Writing this is consciously forcing me to reflect on this, and the answer is yes, I do need to go to the bathroom, but do I stop? No. Why? Because my obsession right now is coming before my basic needs. Neurotypicals may see that as strange or just silly, but it is *normal* for me, and may well be normal for other Autistics too – different, not wrong. I will suppress my basic need to go to the bathroom, until that need becomes too much that it is having an impact on the fulfilling of my obsession. Other people also rely on me to have their needs met; my children, for example. Are my children fed and watered? For reassurance, the answer to this is a resounding yes! Love and guilt drive this as a priority, as does fear of getting into trouble for neglecting my kids! It is *my own* basic needs that tend to get overlooked when I am in full flow obsession.

We can get into such monotropic focus that all else slips away. I forget everything else that matters to me. I must work very hard to ensure those I love are not neglected by my obsessions – my husband and my children – and that includes my business taking over as an obsession, because my business is one hundred percent the product of Autistic obsession. I am yet to come across an Autistic who doesn't have some form of obsession or special interest that isn't fundamental to their being, but as I understand it, there are some Autistics who do not have them. My guess would be that it is rarer than it's common, but again, it is not wrong for an Autistic not to have them.

As for Maslow's Hierarchy of Needs, this is just one of many psychological models that does not fully reflect the experience of Autistic people, but rather the experience of neurotypicals (those of the majority or predominant neurotype). Many of the well-known psychological models that underpin much of today's thinking need to be rethought and revised when it comes to Autistics. The revision needs to be undertaken *by* neurodivergent people *for* neurodivergent people for a truer perspective. **Nothing about us without us**.

The investment we put into our obsessions is obsessive. I can be chit-chatting to my daughter about something I have processed to do with Autism (because of the hours of ruminative thinking I have given to it), and she will

OBSESS ABOUT IT, AND YOU'LL BE SUCCESSFUL AT IT!

just say, "Mum, you are obsessed!" We laugh, because only we as Autistics really know *exactly* what that means. I know it, she knows it. Eighty percent of our conversations centre around Autism, and anyone else would be bored to tears, but we are not, although there *are* times when even she will add, "Mum, you're draining me!" She loves me unconditionally, but around other people I must censor my obsessive interests so as not to bore them, which is all part of my having to mask to not be rejected by neurotypicals, and to fit in. It's not just what I have to mask in, it's also what I must mask or censor *out*.

It's difficult to explain to others just how much thinking I give to my interest topics. I will read about them and think about them constantly. I rarely *stop* thinking about Autism. I think about it when I go running, when I wake in the middle of the night, processing questions and pattern searching for answers. It is non-stop! It is the last thing I think about at night, and the first thing I think about in the morning. And yes, sometimes it *is* exhausting, even for me. The only negative of my obsessions, as I see it, is guilt and rejection. Living for forty-five years undiagnosed autistic, I have internalised many neurotypical ideals, one of which is that, for me as a mother and a wife, my children and my husband, my family, should be the first and last things I think about each day. This is not the case for me, so I feel incredibly guilty for that, yet I do still love my family. I am currently working hard to give myself a different narrative, a neuro-affirming narrative, re-profiling what I am as '*normal* for an Autistic', and to stop holding myself to neurotypical ideals, but this is very much still a work in progress, and I have to be mindful of the impact of my obsessions on those close to me.

As I write now, I am also midway through one of many lived experience books I have been reading about Autism. Learning about Autism and other people's Autistic experiences is enjoyable for me. I visualise what I want to achieve in relation to Autism, what changes I believe are needed. My ultimate desire, above all else, my life's purpose is to help those who are suffering because they are undiagnosed autistic and yet do not know this to find themselves. I don't mean me diagnosing them. I am not a diagnostician and do not have the clinical judgement to do so. What I mean is providing the right information at the right time so that *they* can explore it, work it out for themselves (where it exists), because *they* are the experts in them.

Undiagnosed autistic people will only make the connection if the conditions for that to happen are present, the conditions I referred to previously: 1) self-awareness, 2) searching, or receptiveness to an explanation not yet known, and 3) Autism awareness (non-stereotypical). The part I intend to assist with is number three, one and two are largely outside of my control. Whether the person has the appropriate level of self-awareness, or whether they are searching, or receptive to an explanation not yet known, and whether it is the right time for them will not come down to me. I guess we can help others to be more self-aware, but we can't do it for them. The role I play is in providing information about the female phenotype (presentation) of Autism, about non-stereotypical Autism, through my story and other awareness-raising activity – verbal or written. This is what will drive me for the rest of my living days. Why? Because it is my obsession, and because I am convinced that these are the three conditions required for self-identification. If any are missing, it will simply not happen.

If number **1) self-awareness** is missing, no connection will be made, there simply won't be enough self-awareness on the part of the undiagnosed person to connect with the information in number three.

If number **2) searching, or receptiveness to an explanation not yet known** is missing, I find it can be like throwing playing cards into a fan, and I just have to let it go. If the person is not receptive, there is a reason for this. For example, Autism might not fit with their idea of perfection, and so they resist the connection. It can also sometimes be the case that the person has themselves strongly attached to another label or narrative, e.g., I have an eating disorder, it's menopause, I was adopted, or abused, and this explains everything. Maybe they have made a career, product, or name for themselves on the back of the other label or narrative, they are invested in it, and so their hooks are well and truly attached elsewhere and may not retract. In many cases, these *may* in fact be the explanations for their suffering. But sometimes they over or under attribute or fail to find the true cause and effect. What they miss is that they have *experienced* these other things in such a profound way *because* they are Autistic. They miss another underlying factor. They fight for a cause because Autistics are known for not letting things go, and of course, their cause will often become their obsession, just like my own has, in which case we *definitely* won't let it go, and the cause becomes another of our successes. My own hooks, which were in fact attached elsewhere – in anxiety disorder and gastric problems – when I came across non-stereotypical Autism information, retracted very quickly. The reason for this...? I always knew there was something else missing, they weren't fully attached in the first place.

Sometimes the timing or something else is just not right for the person, and it may never be the right time. Again, that is out of my control. The only thing I have within my control is to keep telling folks and raising awareness of the traits and signs of non-stereotypical Autism, so that, where possible, those who are receptive (most likely the greatest suffering), *will* connect.

I was distinctly missing number **3) Autism awareness (non-stereotypical)** for a very long time, yet one and two were present in abundance. They alone could not create the autistic self-identification I so desperately needed, not without the third and final one. There is, of course, room for fallibility in self-identification, even where all conditions are present, but based on research, many who self-identify their Autism (as opposed to a diagnostician identifying and suggesting it) and then seek diagnosis are rarely wrong. Various studies show adults who self-identified as autistic were very similar to the results of adults with a formal diagnosis of Autism.[26]

OBSESS ABOUT IT, AND YOU'LL BE SUCCESSFUL AT IT!

My obsession with number three – raising awareness of non-stereotypical Autism – means I will share and continue to share my story in various ways: social media, magazines, within my company's training courses, in my books, and pretty much anywhere someone is willing to hear it. It is most definitely an obsession, and I am most definitely obsessive about it. That's all that needs to happen on my part, the rest will happen itself (if the person is autistic and the two other conditions exist). Anything beyond presenting the information to others – for example, attempting to diagnose someone as Autistic – would be totally unethical on my part, a huge breach of boundaries in my professional life and potentially harmful. I am not a diagnostician and wouldn't dream of behaving in a way that I was.

People who connect work it out for *themselves*. They often get in touch with me afterwards, either they come and talk to me, or email me and tell me they can hear themselves in my story. If they are already diagnosed, they tell me they feel less alone in their experience. Where they want more from me after what they learn, they usually ask what the next steps are to getting an assessment, or who assessed me. I have permission from the person who assessed me to share their details with people who ask, but I offer no endorsements. My assistance is more signposting and wishing them all the best with any decision *they* make. A catch and pass approach. Where no connection is made, then the receiver of the non-stereotypical Autism information is either still missing number 1) and/or number 2), or they are not actually Autistic and no connection needs to be made. What *they* instead might take from my story could be something else – passion for a cause, hope, resilience, alliance and understanding of alternative neurotypes, the benefits of perseverance, survival strategies for living in a habitat not built for you, and so on and so forth. They will take from it what is needed and dump the rest or dump it all if they don't see any relevance in any of it. All of that is okay.

I can share my story, placing emphasis on many or any of the key messages I feel will be valuable for the audience, assuming I have been briefed on the audience beforehand, or why I have been asked to share my story or deliver a talk. I find immense value in hearing and reading other Autistic lived experience, how they have survived, and very often, how they are now helping others. It is heartwarming. For a long time, I felt very alone in the world. Today, in the Autistic community, I have people who understand me and understand just as much as I do what it is like to live with an Autistic brain type, or to live undiagnosed for a long time. Through hearing other Autistic lived experience stories and learning about other people's experiences, particularly post-diagnosis, I have recognised that we are very often a mirror to one another. I tend to identify mostly with female and non-binary lived experience, but the book I am currently reading is about a man with Autism, and the way he thinks and works seems to be very similar to the way I do. We are so incredibly different within the spectrum, while being incredibly similar. We can often

OBSESS ABOUT IT, AND YOU'LL BE SUCCESSFUL AT IT!

seem a contradiction in so many ways. You may even see that in such a statement.

Authoring this book is a current temporary obsession situated within a lifetime obsession. I think about it when I am travelling, dream about it, write sections in my head while out running, one obsession feeding the other. The more I run, the more I get into 'the flow' – the brain's alpha state of slower brainwaves, just as might be experienced in meditation – and it's usually when I am at my most creative. I am known to half wake in the middle of the night and write sections of my book into my phone's notes page, tweak something, or jot something down so that my poor working memory doesn't forget it when I fully go back to sleep, *if* I go back to sleep properly, which will depend on how consumed I am. Wherever I am, it happens. I don't force it, I enjoy it, and it just happens. Currently, I am slightly sidetracked from my daytime business obsession, my company Mind Matters, because of my competing Autism obsession, which is overshadowing my obsession with mental health/illness, but at the same time, the two fields overlap considerably, so one obsession still feeds the other. I think of my books as a *product* within my business, a bit like my training courses are the various products we offer. All are educational materials loaded with intention, just in different formats and containing intersectionality.

Because Autistic people (diagnosed and undiagnosed, unidentified and self-identified) can experience lots of challenges, there is a lot of overlap between Autism and mental illness, so the knowledge of each contributes to the knowledge of both. It benefits me and my work to understand both, and to understand other intersections. Since my own diagnosis, I have a theory that most (+50%) cases of mental illness have an unidentified (or identified and waiting to be assessed) aetiology of neurodivergence of some kind – mainly Autism and ADHD, or in some cases both – and people I know working in clinical settings are observing the same. In most cases, one will explain the other, in part, or in full.

I am constantly ruminating over aspects of eating disorders, OCD, personality disorders, and other conditions where there appears to be significant overlap and/or misdiagnosis prior to an Autism (or ADHD) diagnosis. For example, I am currently ruminating over whether some of the personality disorders simply need to be removed from the diagnostic manuals used for diagnosing mental illness, namely the DSM-V and ICD-11? Or whether it is more the case that the professionals diagnosing these conditions need to understand each area better to understand both? Some of the mental health conditions are 'big' diagnoses to give and receive, labels that can lead to stigma and ill treatment of those with the conditions, and not solely from the general public, but sadly from professionals too, like borderline personality disorder (EUPD), for example. I actually think one key question should always be asked and answered *before* any personality disorder diagnosis is given by a mental health diagnostician, and that question is: "Could any of these symptoms also be explained by an underlying neurodivergence such as Autism, ADHD, or both?" If the answer is yes, neurodivergence should be explored first. If the diagnostician cannot answer the question, then they should first consult with someone who can, and *only* then should any personality disorder diagnosis be given. Until we can diagnose this accurately, I believe a moratorium should be placed on diagnosing personality disorders. Potential of a personality disorder diagnosis to do harm is too high a consequence not to. At the moment, mental illness is overshadowing neurodivergence, so people who are neurodivergent are often being diagnosed with the closest fitting mental illness to their traits because the diagnostician they are most likely to find themselves in front of (due to the presence of suffering) is a mental illness professional. The main issue is a lack of non-stereotypical Autism awareness in these professionals, and that needs to change. I mull over such issues for hours and hours and hours, and then some. Searching for the answer becomes a (sometimes frustrating) micro-obsession, and when I feel I have found the answer, it's like my brain and heart want to do a little dance and pop a few (silent) party poppers, but I am held back because I now feel frustrated that things are not changing, or at least not fast enough.

As highlighted, my company, Mind Matters, is without doubt the product of one of my Autistic obsessions – my obsession with mental illness, creating another related obsession – my business. I will tell you more in chapter six about its inception and growth, but its success lies *totally* in it being one of my Autistic obsessions and my being Autistic.

STRENGTH *not* DEFECIT

Autistics will often be great at what they set their minds to, and of what we set our minds to, we can develop an encyclopaedic knowledge. I set my mind to understanding as much as I could take in about mental health and illness. I read widely, I absorbed related facts, and unlike my poor working memory, my ability to recall facts was (is) quite exceptional. Others in my field might even want to emulate this. Please believe me when I say I do not wish to sound showy or arrogant in any way, and I am fully aware I am in danger of doing so. To prove my point, I must illustrate my strengths, and that is my reason for doing so. You can so easily see here why Autistics may become shunned or disliked if they become knowledgeable to the extent that others feel inferior, particularly if they are unfiltered in correcting others, or doing this in social situations that might cause others embarrassment, which is where masking and self-censoring can in fact be helpful. Don't get me wrong, I never ever believe there isn't more to learn – that *would* be arrogant – as we simply do not know what we do not know, but the obsession with which I apply this thinking to my field of work, 'pursuing what I do not know' is, quite simply, obsessive! I love learning, and I love finding answers, but I sometimes struggle to convince others to take the leap of faith with me and believe what I have worked out, especially if there isn't yet something empirical to support my finding. We can often work something out before the science does, so it's then trying to convince others where there isn't an evidence base, or we have to go and create that evidence base ourselves.

OBSESS ABOUT IT, AND YOU'LL BE SUCCESSFUL AT IT!

This is the stage I am at with three theories I have at the moment, and why I plan to return to academia in the next twelve months in the hope of proving (or disproving) what I currently believe to be true. You can see why, historically, Autistic boys were referred to as 'little professors' but you can also see here that there are 'little professor' girls who exist too!

I wonder just how many successful business owners are Autistic (or ADHD, or both) and their successful businesses simply a product of their obsession and Autistic perseverance? How many successful business owners are living undiagnosed because society does not remotely entertain ideas of them being Autistic because they are simply viewed as too successful or too capable?

> NOTE: You are NEVER too successful or too capable to be Autistic. This is just ableism talking.

I see Autistic traits in many highly successful people, in middle-aged women, where my 'neuroscope' is quite active. Now there are two possibilities here, either a hidden population of undiagnosed autistics in high achievement, or the traits of Autism are mirrored in high success, or both(?) – I might even question if they are one and the same? Maybe we share some similarities.

My personal view and one that I put to you is that there is a large hidden population of undiagnosed autistics in high achievers and in the 'successful' business owner community. I am specific when I say 'successful', I am not referring to a hidden population in unsuccessful business owners. You will rarely fail when you put the level of obsession into something that an Autistic who has made it their obsession will, so those who create an unsuccessful business are either not Autistic (not part of the group I am referring to) or their business is *not* in fact their obsession, Autistic obsession or otherwise. I believe obsession is the secret to success, and of successful business ownership, and where you find high-level intense obsession, Autism is also statistically more likely to be present. Don't be fooled by the blind spot, thinking that Autistics are too socially awkward to run businesses and the social demands of business ownership, e.g., networking. Remember, when something is our obsession, we will find ways around the challenging bits. I am not fond of networking by any stretch of the imagination, but I can do it when I need to, when my obsession requires that I do it to achieve a goal or a vision.

Let me illustrate the kind of obsession I am referring to with an example. What if I said to you that, for the next twelve months, I want you to spend twelve hours a day learning to play the clarinet, and you are permitted to have Sundays off, a rest day. I want you to understand the theoretical workings of the clarinet as a musical instrument and I want you to practise playing it during those twelve hours, every day except Sunday. Feel free to put in any extra time you wish, or think about it on your rest day, your day off, think about it all day if you want to. I want playing the clarinet to be the first thing you think about when you wake in the morning, and the last thing you think about at the end of the day before you go to sleep. Assuming you followed my instruction, I would fully expect a high-quality rendition expertly played at the end of the twelve-month period. Make *anything* your obsession and most people will become pretty good at it. Yes, skill does play its part – some will achieve more in that time than others, and some will do it more easily than others – but determination, passion, perseverance and commitment (all features of Autistic obsession) will *always* play a huge and fundamental part in the success. Call it 'grit' if you like. These are the kind of superpowers you will find in high-achieving Autistics, the level at which they will apply to their obsessions, by choice and with pleasure. Do our obsessions become our obsessions because we were good at them, or do we become good at them because they became our obsessions? I'm not entirely sure which comes first, as I think it varies, but my example does not require you to ever have picked up a clarinet in your life, though it may require you to be resourceful to get around the challenges – find and watch YouTube videos, seek out a tutor, maybe manage sores on your fingers or lips, practise, practise, practise, and practise some more. This is the world of my Autistic obsessions. Eat, live, sleep and breathe them, and overcome anything that disables them. The obsession will do this, and success is the outcome.

A business example would be those who succeed at multi-level marketing schemes (MLMs). These are the pyramid model network marketing schemes where the rare few at the top do *very* well, but those further down the pyramid less so (financially speaking). A pyramid because few will obsess to the level that those at the top do, otherwise it would be a different shape! If the majority were obsessive, it would be inverted, for example. Members of such schemes can sell directly, but if they recruit others to sell, and so on and so forth down the pyramid, they receive a commission of the recruits' sales too. If you are financially motivated, this is going to continually bring its own growing motivation. Wouldn't it be interesting to understand who will succeed, who ends up at the top of these schemes? What qualities and characteristics made it possible? Because I am pretty sure it isn't pure luck. Few end up at the top, most scheme members will be in the lower ranks, hence the description of these as 'pyramid schemes'. I believe those at the top will be those who made it their obsession, because obsession will be a key characteristic in those who succeed in these schemes. That obsession brings with it very high determination. Those at the top. They will be tenacious, off-the-charts determined, and every thought or conversation they have, the MLM will be at the forefront of their mind. This is no different to me. So, you may be thinking, is there a disproportionately high number of hidden Autism (or ADHD) at the top of these schemes? I would predict so. I'd expect a high statistical portion of successful MLMers to have ADHD, in fact, more so than Autism. I say this because I generally find those with ADHD are more outgoing and extrovert than Autistics – lots of friends, connections and acquaintances – unless Autism is also present, where I see different dynamics. I met someone recently who had both Autism and ADHD (AuDHD) who felt their ADHD diluted some of their Autistic traits. My daughter has both, and she tends to be less outgoing. I am mindful, of course, that each neurodivergent profile is unique, but patterns do reveal themselves. There may be some Autistics at the top of these schemes, but only if the MLM has become their obsession and they mask well. Autistic level obsession and high social masking would be required to circumvent the social challenges. High social skills are required to work your way to the top of an MLM, there is no room for social awkwardness.

For the successful MLMers, at this point, they have become the least likely to be found. Why? Because their own and others' ableist views will prevent it. They will view themselves and be viewed by others as highly successful and therefore *too* able to be Autistic. I would argue otherwise; the very fact they *are* successful is the indicator they could be. Like those successful in such schemes, in many of my conversations, I am thinking about mental health, Autism, and my company Mind Matters. There is little wonder we make it work. The average entrepreneur likely doesn't do this. That is not a criticism in the slightest, just the reality. Autistics do. And I am not for a moment saying that this is right, or *not* doing so is wrong, I am simply saying that some of us do 'obsession' naturally because of our neurotype, and I believe there is a connection between this obsession and success… and a further connection between success(es) and us being missed.

Some Autistics have made their work or business their obsession, or it became their work or business because it

STRENGTH *not* DEFECIT

became their obsession, and therefore they became better and better at it. As an Autistic, when I am obsessed with something – my business, a book I am writing, a new product or idea – I will be up in the middle of the night because a thought *must* be actioned *right now*. And let's face it, sleep won't happen until we have brain dumped it somewhere. I use my phone, scraps of paper, and if it is possible to action it there and then, I action it there and then, so I don't forget. If I don't, it's gone, my poor working memory will not retain it. And then I will feel incredibly frustrated. I believe Autistics, by nature of a common Autistic trait, are more likely to operate this level of obsession than a neurotypical might. This level of obsession is rarely considered 'normal' by neurotypical standards because it is not what *most* people do.

Societal ideas of what is 'normal' in any area of our life is what sets Autistics apart. Our Autism can, in many areas, be illustrated by the way we are situated on the fringes of what society deems as 'normal'. I am confused when I hear statements such as, "Well, what is normal anyway?" as I believe Autistics are some of the outliers that illustrate perfectly well what society deems and accepts as 'normal'. I am an Autistic who socially masks, so I must know what 'normal' is as I apply it daily, and it's the very reason you (and everyone else) didn't know I was Autistic for forty-five years, and why most people don't know I am Autistic until I tell them. It has never been an illusion for me – I've always known I don't 'fit in', that I am 'different' – it's an illusion for you, to convince *you* that I do, not for me. At

OBSESS ABOUT IT, AND YOU'LL BE SUCCESSFUL AT IT!

the very least, to be effective in this, I need to know what is accepted as 'normal' by society, otherwise what exactly am I to mimic? My social masking wouldn't exist without an understanding of 'normal'. So yes, we do know what 'normal' is. The issue with 'normal' is that it has been defined by neurotypicals for neurotypicals, not by Autistics for Autistics; my 'normal' looks different to neurotypical 'normal', but it's 'normal' for me. Judge me by the norms of an Autistic and I am *totally* normal. Autistics didn't make Autism the outlier, society did.

Here are just some of the outliers that, unless I share them with you, you won't ever know about me, but that *do* reveal me as 'different' and always did:

My first marriage... I was married to a man twenty years and six months my senior – that is *not* 'normal' by neurotypical standards, is it? Society does not see large age gap marriages as 'normal'. You'll hear comments regarding ulterior motives such as money, one of the partners having it and the other not (my husband nor I had money, so that wasn't the attraction), midlife crisis (that one I cannot rule out in one of us) and others. I knew it was not viewed as normal or acceptable from the outset due to the reactions from neurotypicals to it at the time, and even now when I share it there can be a few raised eyebrows. Viewed through an Autistic lens, you may learn that Autistics don't have the same issues with age that neurotypicals might, and we also tend to connect really well with those outside of our own age group. So, through an Autistic lens, it's much more normal.

STRENGTH *not* DEFECIT

> Note: the marriage ended a long time ago, but I have remarried, and my current husband is thirteen years my junior.

Autistics are a great example of pushing the boundaries of what is deemed 'normal'; what is normal for us is often *not* normal by neurotypical standards.

Becoming a grandmother at thirty-six... My daughter was 'planned' pregnant at fifteen. Of course, not with my knowledge at the time, because this exceeds even my own boundaries and standards, but look at this through an Autistic lens and you will see a desperate search for identity, in this case in motherhood. Teenage pregnancy, while not rare, is still *not* seen as 'normal' by lots of people's standards, it is frowned upon. I do wonder how much of it might be explained through undiagnosed Autism, ADHD, or both?

Workaholism... Being overly obsessed with your work is not seen as normal or acceptable either, you are referred to as a workaholic. Work is viewed as a means to live, not living for those means, but what if your work is your Autistic obsession? Workaholism is seen as negative, pathologised in conditions such as obsessive compulsive personality disorder, where it is viewed as a symptom. But again, view it through an Autistic lens, what in my own case would be seen as workaholism, is in fact my Autistic obsession. You'll see here one of several reasons why I thought I had OCPD prior to my Autism diagnosis.

If you want to find us, just look at extremes of anything, behaviours that push the boundaries of acceptance, and

OBSESS ABOUT IT, AND YOU'LL BE SUCCESSFUL AT IT!

you'll find us there hiding in plain sight – the outliers. I've seen enough side-eye and raised eyebrows in my lifetime to know exactly what society accepts and doesn't, and that's the very reason I socially mask. It is, of course, underpinned by never feeling safe in a majority neurotypical society. Other societal examples might include those who have families of sixteen children, extreme weight loss and gain, visual extremes such as full body tattooing. Some of this I see more in those with ADHD or where the person is Autistic *and* has ADHD, such as my daughter – tattoos, piercings and coloured hair. They may seem like visual extremes to neurotypicals but not to those of us with ADHD or Autism. Extremes of difference is one of the ways my own 'neuroscope' spots other Autistic people. Sometimes it is quite a visual thing, other times it's behaviours I pick up on, how they hold their arms, their shoulders and neck, how they speak, or don't speak, or how they communicate. There is often an extreme about them, or one (or more) in their life story, a pattern, something that illustrates them as an outlier of societally accepted norms. Sometimes it's these very extremes that become our successes (neurotypical ideas of success that is, the benchmark I said I would use for this book) – extreme skill, knowledge, talent – and the subsequent success that tends to follow. This I see in some of the most successful and talented celebrities, their success visible in the very fact that they 'made it' – driven by determination and underlying obsession – but where there is often some indication of suffering too. The suffering is telling you more if you are willing to listen to it.

My own life extremes are what astonish me today that my family and I weren't identified Autistic sooner. I can socially mask all I like, but the moment I share my 'outliers', you'll see the 'difference' – but again, if you don't have non-stereotypical Autism awareness you will miss it just the same. I want to be crystal clear here in saying that none of these differences are wrong, not in my opinion anyway, they just show how we are 'different' from most people in society. We are normal for Autistics. I am simply saying it is not what *society* accepts as 'normal'. Society judges it, sometimes very harshly, and I believe society is sometimes confused and frightened by 'difference', even when you give the 'difference' a label like Autism; maybe more so when you give it a label? I think society is scared of us. If you want to find people who are much less likely to judge us, it's us, Autistics. Why would we ever judge 'difference' when most of the time it is us being judged for being different? Many Autistics have felt the negative impact of that, which can in some cases simply cause us to hide our difference, or to accelerate our difference – if we cannot 'fit in', we just 'fit out' more.

What other business owners (or wannabe business owners) could learn from successful Autistics, and successful Autistic business owners: If you want to make your business venture a success, simply make it your obsession. If you are not already good at what you do, you will become good at it by way of obsessing. Do this at least until the business reaches critical mass – the point at which a self-sustaining rate is reached – where the momentum

OBSESS ABOUT IT, AND YOU'LL BE SUCCESSFUL AT IT!

you have given should start to drive itself. For higher levels of success, the early years will require the kind of effort equivalent to Autistic obsession. If you cannot do this, work with someone who can, but you will need to be mindful of the 'give-receive' balance in partnerships. One won't do all the work and let the other sit with their feet up for long, so what is going to be your contribution? Essentially, eat, live, sleep and breathe it… and then some! Neurotypicals have a benefit that I don't have here. Neurotypicals will be able to dial up or dial down their obsession level. When my obsessions form, they are not given a dial. I don't have such control over them. At best, I can mask them where they are viewed negatively in any way.

CHAPTER 6

Making Something from Nothing; Ignoring the Naysayers and Autistic Perseverance

My business, Mind Matters, has grown organically, driven by (a lot) of Autistic obsession. Prior to its inception, I had stepped away from another business, for a variety of reasons, a business that had once been my obsession too, and which had reached critical mass by the time I left, and still exists now. It too was a product of obsession.

At the point of departure, my plan was to take things slowly, and as I iterated to others, to "Stop and smell the roses for a while." Who was I fooling!? I have never yet stopped and smelt the bloody roses! And my general feeling is that, while people are out there suffering and there's work to be done, I likely never will. I don't know how to stop, but today I do know 'why' – my being Autistic. I am rarely able to fully shut down when away from my work. The thoughts just jump back in. This is because I cannot let something go, and when I become impassioned about something, it consumes me and easily becomes an obsession. One of the things that drives me and my business, and in fact my life's purpose, is to help to reduce suffering in other people where I can, either directly, or indirectly through my work, life and values. This is what makes me tick. It wasn't these things that caused the initial inception of my business, however, or not consciously so. They were just the given that has always been there – the bedrock – intrinsic to who I am.

In early June 2015, I was attending a social media training course at a local storage centre, held in their training room facility. The course was for my husband's IT business, the so-called 'stopping and smelling the roses' interlude in my life (which lasted a month!), which was helping him out with his accounts administration and a bit of business marketing. May I remind you here that I have suspected dyscalculia, a grade E in GSCE maths, and my junior school maths teacher used to give me points for putting my name on the exam paper! My oversight could be forgiven since, at this point in my life, I was still in the 'I have no limits' pre-diagnosis stage. The bigger oversight here is that my husband's business is *not* my obsession, and unlikely to become one, so it would render unlikely that I am going to get around the challenges because I would not be highly motivated or determined to do so.

> Note: Obsession has the power to overcome disability because it is loaded with determination. If I had no obsessions, and therefore no achievements and success, you would only see my disabilities, and think me a deficit.

Obsession is the key, it is fuelled by determination – just like the fires of hell lashing at your behind – but perhaps disappointing for my husband, and his business partner, their IT business was *not* my obsession. It would have been convenient if it had been, but you can't just make an Autistic obsession happen, it's organic.

So, at the training course, in addition to learning about optimal use of social media, I got chit-chatting to the course trainer about the room and the practicalities of how to hire it, including associated costs. At this point, the embers of something were starting. I was pondering training courses and clearly entertaining ideas that maybe, just maybe, I could run a mental health training course at the site. It was most definitely affordable, I was already qualified from my previous work, and was organised and motivated enough to make it happen. Flame ignited.

I am a qualified mental health trainer, qualified to deliver a number of licensed mental health training courses, at that time mainly Mental Health First Aid. Working for my husband's business, I was hugely missing my vocation and life's purpose of helping to ease suffering. The previous business I had developed, with a business partner, focused on mental health, and I was missing making a positive difference to those with mental health difficulties. The biggest question in front of me now was: Did I, Jane McNeice, have the confidence to give it a go? Confidence was, and still is, my weak spot. I shouldn't even write that, or think it, otherwise I risk self-fulfilling prophecy. I am counter-thinking now *I can, I can, I can* before anything less embeds. Late diagnosis narrative is dominant in my vernacular and often needs to be silenced quickly! A manager in my first ever job at the age of sixteen had a phrase she regularly asserted, "Do it, and wonder how you did it afterwards." It kind of stuck and so that's what I did.

I entertained the idea some more, spoke with my husband, and the bones of something started to come together. With vision, things began to materialise, one step at a time. At some point during this time, my business obsession, Mind Matters, was borne.

Obsession leads to action, determined machine-like action, and from there came a basic website from which I could advertise the courses, and from which I would go on to create content and articles, which I still do today, content from which I can gain much mileage. For example, I blog. That blog can then be circulated, reused when a relevant topic pops up on social media, or in other outlets, all because the hard work was done (once). It can be used in our digital newsletter, which goes out quarterly nowadays, due to the volume of actual training deliveries preventing the more regular monthly publishing. One blog, lots of capital. This kind of stuff is what I call 'throwing muck at the wall', or what my husband prefers to call 'throwing sh*t at the wall'. Please do not underestimate the effort therein, it is just a crude reference to dogmatic perseverance and determination, which I will talk more about later in the chapter. Each written piece is well thought out (*over* thought out), crafted from the heart, checked twice, thrice and four times, and is totally driven by my own and my company's values, which are aligned and operational in everything we do. My company's values were not written on the back of a matchbox but were and are a true representation of what we are about, what we are trying to achieve and how. They are borne of one overarching intention: **Reducing suffering in others.** What I had failed to realise prior to my diagnosis, however, is that to do this *effectively*, I had to reduce suffering in someone else – me – and today, post diagnosis, those two concepts are also much more united. My own self-care is integral to my company's achievements. The likelihood of my continued efforts being successful is much greater *knowing* I am Autistic, because now I fully recognise and acknowledge that my need for self-care is the top priority, and without it the other bits won't happen. My self-care had to be increased.

For a long time, I would not use the word 'success' to describe my business, but in the last year I have slowly come round to the idea that what I have achieved is something special. This shift coincides with a slow building of self-esteem and self-worth, which also started at diagnosis in June 2021. This second book would not have materialised without that shift because it's a book that demonstrates (and celebrates) the strengths and achievements, not the deficits, and prior to diagnosis I couldn't truly acknowledge that what I had achieved was something successful, and a product of my strengths.

Now of course, I fully appreciate that 'success' is a subjective concept; what is successful to one person is not to the next. There are, of course, the neurotypical ideals and trappings of success – money, status, company size, employee numbers, etc. Perhaps they are the measures of success for some neurodivergents too. But not this one, not anymore, though there was a time when they would have been. Back then, though, they were driven by perfection, in part a perfection driven by the need to impress others because I never felt very good about myself. Today, anything you may see as successful in me or my company is driven by healthy intention, and it's important to understand the difference. Healthy intention means that everything I do comes from a healthy place, a healthier state of mind, and aims to bring about good. If my business *does* make money, that money can be used to reduce even more suffering in even greater ways. It gives me choices; it can buy me a platform to a greater audience and make the difference-making happen in greater volumes. Financial reward isn't dirty in and of itself, quite clean in fact, if it is put to greater good and betterment of the world. Even before my diagnosis, I have always viewed financial reward as a by-product of what we do in my company, not the reason for, and I always come back to the same place of intention – we want to reduce suffering, that of mental and emotional ill health, which has an impact on people physically, and an impact on those around them. Today, I am aware that the Autistic community, my community, are overrepresented in those that suffer mental illness.

So, we started out with a basic website and planned our first course, scraping together the odd free delegate place to meet the minimum delegate numbers set by the course licensor, MHFA England, and delivered on a tight budget. Room hired, resource packs at the ready, bottles of water, stationery, and a nice buffet lunch. We had the people in the room, my anxiety through the roof, and as Susan Jeffers would say, "felt the fear and did it anyway."[27] My ability to do this, despite the challenges, existed because what we do at Mind Matters makes a difference to reducing suffering in others and is driven by Autistic obsession!

> Note: it is passion for a cause and determination that allows me to overcome my low confidence, anxiety and gastric problems that would otherwise disable me and prevent me from delivering training. Determination and perseverance are the Autistic USP, impelled further when driven by Autistic obsession. Lack of confidence is one of my greatest challenges, but my level of determination overcomes this.

Two things were now operating together, both fuelled by obsession – the actual mental health course deliveries and the constant marketing that brings attention to our courses. My company used all the free software offerings until we reached a point where we had to pay, and I paid where the cost benefit of a particular software was worth it. We slowly afforded better marketing materials, shared with our stakeholders the different things we were doing, free resources and the like, and I delivered to the absolute best of my Autistic obsession and ability. When volumes reached a stage where my own capacity was running thin,

I found others who shared our values and vision, and first came my wing-woman Gemma-Skye, who delivers many courses for us each year. Gemma also delivers with purpose, wants to save lives, and brings all the beauty of her own neurodivergence to her course deliveries. Beyond Gemma, we have recruited other associate trainers who believe in what we do, and the difference-making of mental health training courses, and now have a team of people as committed as we are. We value neurodiversity and other diversities in our associate pool. They are a great team.

> Note: not all our associate trainers are neurodivergent, many are neurotypical, because it wouldn't be very neurodiverse to have a pool of only neurodivergent associate trainers. And, as we accept neurodivergence is a variant not a fault, we must also accept that neurotypical is not faulty. No one brain type is superior to another, and heterogeneity is favoured over homogeneity. To be clear, I mean any group of people made up of ALL neurotypes, not just one, is best.

Neurodiversity is not the only diversity in our team. Our associate pool is made up of a variety of other diversities, and in terms of the pool of experience, some have a corporate working background, some have had and still have roles in mental health services, some have a human resources background, and they all share one common theme. *All* are very talented. Some also have their own businesses as

STRENGTH *not* DEFECIT

well as their associate work with us, and many are 'lived experience' trainers. We don't come to the 'helping' work that we do by accident; in most cases, it comes to us because we need to make good of our own pain. You take your own pain, and you try to ease and prevent it in others through purpose that aids this. Like my associate trainers, I too offer myself out for associate opportunities, which offers personal credibility via the other amazing organisations that I am privileged to work with. One thing we are always attempting to prove to our prospective clients is that you can trust us, put your faith in our services, we are safe to work with, our products are safe to work with, and we are credible. When they have worked with us, they learn that that is true.

At the start of a client journey, there is a lot of unspoken asking of people to trust you, and sometimes I will put my money where my mouth is, allowing them to test us out, a bit like when supermarkets let you try out a sample before you buy. Trust can be a difficult thing to achieve (and so very easily lost forever), so sticking your neck out with an offering communicates that I am willing to go where you are and to prove it to you. Some of our long-standing clients are those who trusted us early on, and who we have not let down both in reliability and in quality, one recently providing a reference to our work and stating they had been offered *free* services similar to our paid-for services, but declined them in favour of us.

In my book *The Umbrella Picker*, I talk about a group of people I refer to as 'alpha-neurotypicals' or 'alpha-socials', those for whom 'social' comes as natural to them as breathing. I talk about my attraction to these people as I learn so much from them and I describe my youngest son Ben as one of these. He teaches me how to be more sociable every single day and has been able to make friends better than I can since he was three, maybe even younger. As my own knowledge of neurodivergence and neurodiversity is expanding – through obsession in, and with, the literature and narrative in both areas – I am starting to see that maybe I was wrong, the 'alpha-socials' were *not* in fact 'alpha-socials' but rather people with ADHD, or certain types of ADHD.

I have a theory that Autistics might often develop partner and friend relationships with those with ADHD, as the two are likely to come together when the more outgoing ADHDers reach out to the less socially confident Autistics, who they seem to connect well with because they are both neurodivergent. This leaves us simply to reciprocate, which is a lot easier for Autistics than initiating friendships, which many of us find difficult. I believe my current husband to have undiagnosed ADHD and have solid theories on all my past key relationships, not just intimate relationships, but key business relationships too. My husband was the one who initiated our relationship. I would never have done so due to lack of social confidence. I have never ever asked anyone out on a date or ever initiated a friendship. I am too socially awkward to do so, and do not know how. I have either been asked and reciprocated, a third party became involved or was involved in the initiation, or the relationship was brought together through common purpose, e.g., work, and it went from there. Common purpose can really help me to create relationships where otherwise it would not happen. Most of my close friendships were born from common purpose; we worked or studied together in the first instance. Common purpose is part of how I have built relationships with my clients and learners.

Referring to my youngest, whether it *is* possible that Ben has ADHD, the big conundrum for myself and my husband right now, my books will certainly illustrate one thing… the changes and development in my youngest son since 2021 when he was five, the age at which these conditions start to present in our own family which seems to be age seven, but also the constant development and expanding of my own knowledge on neurodivergence. And I would expect this. I am constantly questioning and seeking to understand more, so progressive learning *should* be expected over time. In relation to my field of work, mental health training, I have a view that of *all* the neurotypes, there would likely be a higher number of mental health trainers who have ADHD than who are Autistic, particularly those with the hyperactive-impulsive type, rather than the inattentive type, and more so where extroversion is also their personality type. I generally believe there are likely to be more extroverts who are trainers than introverts. However, it's important to say here that the lines are not clear cut on ADHD types, introversion and extroversion. There is a lot of intersectionality, including between ADHD and Autism, which is why some people with ADHD also connect with my story – they connect with the overlap between the two conditions, or they have both conditions – so no absolute assumptions should be made. It's also a possibility that there are more activists who are trainers. I think you are far less likely to find a trainer who is Autistic, very introverted, and a theorist like me, but all the same, I am a working example of the fact that it *is* possible and possible to be successful at it – strength not deficit – but it does need the vital ingredient of obsession to overcome the challenges that would otherwise prevent it. The training room is a socially demanding environment for an Autistic, especially navigating the small talk that happens at the beginning and during break times.

So, what then makes it possible for an Autistic to deliver training courses? What does me being obsessed with something have the power to do that gets around the challenges that would ordinarily prevent it?

The secret is the determination that goes with obsession, which translates as having to work harder than others might, but having the energy to do so because it is obsessive. As an Autistic, I have a strong need to be in control. A training room is a much more controlled environment than you might initially think, especially if you can rule out as many of the unknowns as possible. One fear that many trainers have is not being able to answer a question. I don't have this fear because I'm not frightened of saying I don't know the answer either. The fears *I* have are different, they are more social. An Autistic who delivers training in a subject of their obsession will make it their place to ensure they know a lot about the subject, so not knowing the answer rarely happens. If there is a question they don't know the answer to, and you put that to an Autistic whose obsession it is, they too will now want to know the answer, especially because it is in their field of interest. They will want to provide an answer for you *and* for themselves, and you can be sure they will go off and find it out. I will absorb as much information and research as possible about mental health, but (hopefully) never be so arrogant to think I know it all, even though I recognise that sometimes we are viewed that way by neurotypicals who don't fully understand us or why we seem to know a lot. I read about mental health, research it, watch documentaries, and watch and listen to people's narrative about it, for pleasure! This is not so I can answer every question that I am confronted with in the training room, it is because of my thirst for mental health knowledge.

Autistics wanting to reduce their anxiety will rule out as many unknowns as possible. We like things to be predictable, it helps us to feel safe. Reducing the anxiety starts with absorbing knowledge, but also includes extensive plans for getting to the venue, managing time and overcompensating for travel problems or other unknowns, to the point where I have moved most things which would otherwise be out of my sphere of control, into it. Historically, this would have been referred to as being a 'control freak' but today I know it instead as the Autistic discomfort with lack of predictability and a need for routine, something all Autistics experience to a greater or lesser extent. I have a very internal locus of control. I don't expect others to do it for me, I take my own responsibility for my life and can foresee problems much more quickly than most. I've never had the support, so I've got used to not having it, doing things for myself, and being independent. This sort of planning then leaves very little outside of my control, and what is left outside of my control I am quite capable of accepting. I shift to acceptance very quickly, quicker than most other people do in fact, but only when I know something is clearly out of my control. I also say to myself, *What is the worst that can happen?* This is usually enough to manage any catastrophising, and one of the few cognitive behavioural therapy techniques that I *have* found beneficial, though it did not come from a therapy room, it came from a colleague I worked with in the early noughties who used to say this. All these things I have had no choice but to learn to do – sink or swim – because living undiagnosed Autistic for forty-five years means I did not get the support I should have had when it was needed, so instead I learned ways of supporting myself. It was always about survival, and still is.

My knowledge and fact recall are exceptional, and once I have delivered a training product several times, I will have developed an Autistic script for it. Autistic scripting is a form of Autistic masking, where we memorise dialogue, strings of words and sentences, and regurgitate them as required. I am good at remembering the best lines from lots of things and reciting them when it's needed. Provided I continue to deliver a course regularly, it simply becomes very embedded in my neural pathways. Once it is, I can play with the script to greater benefit. It doesn't mean I cannot go 'off script' as my wide knowledge of mental health allows for this, but having done so, I regress back to the predictability and safety of the script, and the structure of the course. Wide knowledge of the subject matter is always my fail-safe. If my fail-safe *is* failing, it is quite simply because I don't know enough about the topic or subject matter on which I am speaking, and I must go back to the learning and increase it. So, as you will see, one of my coping mechanisms is to know everything I can about a subject. If I am daunted by a subject, I simply learn as much as I possibly can about it.

The things I must work hardest at are the things it is impossible to predict; for example, a name belonging to a certain face. I do not know this until I am in the training room; it is out of my sphere of control until that point and connecting the two repeatedly during a course (when it *is* in my control) requires a good working memory. I do not have a very good working memory, I have a good *long-term* memory, so one of my other coping mechanisms has been to become proficient at anchoring.

Anchoring is a memory aid, often used by memory masters, to memorise things. It does as its name suggests, you anchor one thing to another. Anchoring is often linked to the various senses. I anchor visually. I anchor the person's name and face to a third thing (visual or circumstance), and this is how I remember them. Sometimes it's a funny thing, like X looks like my mother-in-law, or Y looks like so-and-so on TV. Unconsciously, I third anchor to the setting, in this case the room we are in. Failure to do this means I simply won't remember, and it will cause me to feel embarrassed and to appear as if I don't care when actually I *really* care, a lot. Again, my fears are socially based, the things others find easy (or easier). Anchoring isn't infallible. For instance, if I anchor to something that is transient and might change (usually the third anchor), or I fail to predict it will change. Like when you then see the same person in a supermarket or not in a uniform, and you anchored them to a seat in a room, or to a uniform, and you cannot now fathom who they are. Even when I successfully anchor someone to something, I might still struggle with the face. I am most definitely aware that I have some element of face-blindness with my Autism – prosopagnosia – as I just cannot recognise many faces, especially out of context, and remembering names is my nemesis. If I am delivering my training online and people keep cameras off, I find this extremely difficult, but not impossible. This is an interesting one because I have recently read online that many Autistics prefer their own cameras to be 'off' as a reasonable adjustment for online meetings or training. Whose Autistic needs should be met when the Autistic trainer needs the cameras on, and an Autistic learner needs theirs off? That's an easy one for me to answer in terms of my training courses – my learner's need would supersede my own – but what if that was two learners both requiring their individual needs to be met? It's trickier as we then get into whose need is greater and the legal test of 'reasonableness' for adjustment has competition in terms of the 'practicality' test and the impact of the adjustment on others. We would also need to consider the four other tests, which conclude whether an adjustment is in fact 'reasonable' for each, and to do so objectively. Failure to do this correctly might put you in front of an employment tribunal who will certainly give you their answer, with a possible penalty if you chose wrongly. Another illustration that, even as an Autistic community, with common traits, we all have different needs, and to various degrees.

Providing instructions isn't my strong point either, so I always check for understanding and offer clarity because I am aware that if it doesn't sound clear in my own head, it is unlikely to be clear for my learners also. Post-diagnosis, I can now explain myself a little more to my audience, and while there are many Autistics who say we shouldn't have to apologise for who (or how) we are, I still have times when I see it as necessary, especially if it is having an impact on my learners' experience, my business and therefore my obsession.

> Note: I did not say I can't provide instruction, I just said I must find alternative routes to the same outcome. Sometimes it is as simple as showing some vulnerability to generate increased compassion and support from your audience; you can't expect them to be mind readers. A beautiful thing I have learned in the last eight years is that most people do care, and that was something I really did need to learn.

My company training portfolio grew, in diversity and in volume, and today we are still expanding, increasingly offering courses around neurodivergence, and helping others to recognise how neurodivergence can have an impact on mental health. I am today of a mindset that we need to stop seeing these two fields as totally separate, we need to look at the intersectionality, we need to understand fully what and why that is, and we need to find the missing Autistics to have the fullest understanding. Only if we understand both can we understand each. The challenge is that, historically, we have focused on increasing mental health awareness in such a purist way that other conditions which have a huge impact, or can underpin, have been overlooked. We have increasingly recognised the links between mental ill health and LGBTQIA+ and race, but not yet accepted the overlap with Autism and mental illness in the same way. There is also intersectionality within all said areas.

We know, for example, that there is a disproportionately high number of undiagnosed autistics in the transgender or gender-diverse community,[28] so to support one section of people could be to intersectionally support another. I'm liking that I've just spotted 'ally' at the end of intersection**ally**, because when you support one, one does in fact become an ally to the other – to support trans people can be to support Autistic people, and vice versa. There is a possibility that identifying as trans, or gender-diverse, may in some cases (but not in all) blind the person to other unidentified identities in the form of either Autism,

ADHD, or both, where they also exist in the same person. I want to make a point here in saying that in no way am I denying or invalidating their other identities.

Autism is an identity just like identifying as trans or gender-diverse, or another identity. Trans and gender-diverse identities might be examples of identities that someone is so well attached to that it closes their mind to other considerations, additional identities, and in doing so prevents number **2) searching, or receptiveness to an explanation not yet known** in my criteria for self-identification from being realised; that is, they are not 'receptive to a truth not yet known' or '*another* truth not yet known'. They already believe the answer is found for their sense of 'difference'. Attachment to another identity which offers a sense of belonging and a supportive community can reduce any searching or receptiveness to another identity which can afford the same, or even more self-identity and awareness. This could be said of other identities also, and of other labels, including menopause. We attach ourselves to one label and the accompanying narrative, and this can create a blind spot elsewhere. I am aware of this in my own case too.

Am I so attached to my Autism label, narrative and identity that I link *everything* to it, and in doing so miss something else, now, or at some stage in the future? Maybe a symptom that is linked to something else, which I mistakenly connect with Autism? I believe that I could, but I am hopeful that in knowing that's a possibility, being conscious of it, I will be curious, second question, or third question, so I am no longer blind to it. I remind myself that some of the things I experience *could* be explained by other things unrelated to my being Autistic; something linked to menopause, for example, or another form of neurodivergence. Yes, I have entertained the possibility of me having another unidentified neurodivergence – ADHD – and so I have explored it, discounted it, clinically too, to be sure; I only have Autism. I explored it because I do have some ADHD traits – caffeine relaxes me, I talk fast, I am constantly restless, and others – but they wouldn't likely meet the threshold for an ADHD diagnosis, they are simply part of my neurodivergent profile, and reflective of an overlap between neurodivergent conditions. If you can accept you have blind spots, you can be conscious of them, and when you are conscious of them, you can seek to expose them. But you will never find them all, that is the ultimate blind spot.

I had for a long time attached myself to a narrative of 'managed anxiety disorders and gastric problems' (creating a blind spot elsewhere) until someone questioned why the anxiety and gastric problems needed a lot of management and had never gone away, which motivated me to go back to the searching and exploring with more vigour. The person showed me I had allowed myself a blind spot, even though that wasn't their direct intention. The person was merely curious and musing about my symptoms.

Failure to recognise the overlap in these identities and conditions with Autism – the blind spot for professionals – manifests in damage, that of misdiagnosis, which appears to be prolific, and which I talk more about in my memoir *The Umbrella Picker*. Those with the clinical judgement to diagnose mental illness have not, in most cases, been given sufficient knowledge around neurodivergent conditions, such as Autism and ADHD, and the intersections therein, which is why many of us received misdiagnoses of mental illnesses before our truth was found. Had the professionals who diagnosed my mental illnesses have been Autism alert, to the signs and presentation of Autism in girls, women (and non-binary), then I would have received the correct diagnosis much earlier, with an acknowledgement that my anxiety is in fact a co-existing symptom of my being Autistic, rather than me having anxiety disorder(s) and being mentally ill per se. I have no objection in receiving a mental health diagnosis, and much of my work centres around reducing the stigma surrounding mental illnesses and diagnosed mental illness, but I *do* object to inaccurate labels (and the resulting consequences of less effective treatment) where it leaves someone suffering, and especially when it leaves them thinking they have something *wrong* with them! The two areas need to stop operating in silos and need to pool knowledge and experience to greater benefit. Mental health needs to stop overshadowing neurodivergence to its detriment, and conversely, to the detriment of mental health.

Today my own business is being shaped with that in mind, to be the change I want to see in the clinical world. I think Mind Matters is at the forefront of change in doing this, an early adopter, where many providers are still purist mental health training providers. I am smiling because as an Autistic who struggles with change, I am *rarely* ever an early adopter of anything! It is rare that I come across people working in mental health who have a sound knowledge and understanding of mental health *and* neurodivergence, but when I do, it is wonderful! They often have so much insight to share. I follow some of these amazing people on the professional social media platform LinkedIn – Jackie Schuld and Hayley Graham, to name just a couple. Their number will grow in time, I feel sure of it.

There are many statistics that illustrate the unfortunate failure rate of new business start-ups, which is cited as 60% failure in the first three years.[29] I didn't entertain any of this thinking during the development years, to avoid anything self-fulfilling, but I also didn't describe what I had achieved as successful either. I just pushed on.

Not everyone close to me shared the same belief in what I was doing, or in my ability to achieve it. This hurt incredibly at the time, and as I have an exceptional emotional memory, I still feel it now. I've come across many 'naysayers' in my life, but what naysayers do for me is bring out my perseverance even more – it's like a red rag to a bull when someone tells me, or intimates, I won't achieve something; I also link this to my being Autistic. It's the same when I see someone trying to belittle others or making fun of someone else's difficulties. I guess it's somewhere between stubbornness, perseverance, a constant drive to feel and be worthy and the discomfort I experience when seeing others suffer at the hands of bullies. Someone close to me had said my business would never be a success, it would never be financially viable (failing to recognise money wasn't in fact my driver or my measure of success), and though they have never retracted this verbally, they now recognise they were wrong. They recognised they misjudged both it and me at the time. I sense nowadays that they are *very* wary to question anything I say I am going to do. In fact, they haven't questioned anything since.

I had similar smiles and smirks from people when I said I was going to run the London marathon, my ambitions seen as lofty and perhaps above my station. Red rag to a bull. I ran it two years in succession, but not for them – for good intention – for me, and for the National Autistic Society, to raise much needed charitable funds for Autistic people. I also believe there is a disproportionate number of hidden undiagnosed autistics in runners, especially long-distance runners, and people who have run marathons. To run a marathon takes high levels of perseverance – the Autistic USP. Where many would 'throw the towel in' and give up, we won't. Marathon running, or running several marathons, is a socially acceptable outlier, so any connection with Autism is overlooked. It's an extreme most people won't have the desire, obsession, or perseverance to do. It sits outside of 'normal' running distances that most people might do for exercise. There are far fewer people who do it than you might perceive when you watch the TV coverage of the London marathon, for example. Throughout the world, only about 1.1 million runners finish a marathon each year, which equates to 0.01% of the global population.[30] Put simply, not many! When Autistics are told we cannot... we so often can, and will! My late brother proved we should ignore the 'naysayers', he worked it out well before I did.

The things I become obsessed about feature in my brain most of the time and are often linked to an outcome I desire. That outcome will be visual, as I have a very image-based brain. I see pictures, patterns, connections and systems, often web-like. I will always have a vision of the end game, and this vision is usually very detailed and prominent in my mind. I believe this is also key to my ability to materialise a desire. If there is no vision, I am not ready yet, and it won't come to fruition. I currently have a vision for this book, it is unfolding, and I am constantly drawing back to the vision and the big picture, a bit like looking at the jigsaw box cover when putting a jigsaw together.

One of the reasons I need to go back to the big picture is because I experience the central cohesion problems that many Autistics experience. I have my eye so fixed on the bow and arrow I can sometimes fail to notice the target and where it is situated. I focus on the detail at the cost of not fully comprehending the big picture or meaning, so I need a visual reminder of where I am aiming. An eye for detail is a great skill – being able to spot something others may miss, for example, or seeing the beauty in something that others might not – but I need to see the big picture too. The risk with my book here is that I get so lost in the detail that I lose the overall point and aim of a chapter, or even the whole book, one of which is *not* to repeat the words of my previous memoir and to end up with another version of the same! I want my books to stand alone but enhance each other if you happen to have read both. My lived experience in this book is background information for context, whereas my lived experience was central to my previous book. At times, my central cohesion is dragging me back to my lived experience and losing sight of the big picture.

For a vision to materialise, and to stay on track, it requires strategy and goals, but they need to be clearly aligned with the vision. I need a strong anchor between the big vision I am aiming for, which is fuelled by obsession, and that of the detail. It is the obsession and my keeping stepping back to the big picture that will knit it together. If I don't do this regularly enough, I run the risk of mission drift and the aims of the book will be lost!

CHAPTER 7

All Ideas Are Borne Inside Our Heads

I am known to wander off into my head and stay there for quite some time. Those who know me will know 'the look'. It looks quite vacant, but that is so far from the truth of what is happening cerebrally. I have totally switched off from my surroundings and I am immersed instead in whatever it is that my brain is processing and creating.

From early childhood, I always had some kind of project in motion, a club with membership goodies, or other attractions, a club that did not go on to seek any members, and which I was okay with. I took great pleasure in the development of clubs but had very little interest and investment in the next step. While today my business outcomes and success require me to work on all steps – development through to marketing and delivery – I often have some project or idea in the pipeline, just the same as in childhood. Sometimes it is a project within a project, a micro-obsession. I love the process, sometimes I love the process more than the end product. The process gives me the rosy glow rather than the completion. My business

Mind Matters is perhaps my biggest project yet, but there are and have been, many which have existed within it.

Currently, one of our most important projects is the shift from purist mental health training to including training around neurodivergence and neurodiversity because of the significant overlap therein, and so that we can lead where others might follow, being the change we want to see. We are also introducing an additional suicide intervention programme to the Mind Matters training portfolio and the whole 'project' that is Suicide First Aid – upskill training, assignments, observations, marketing, and lastly, but most importantly, the delivery of excellence so that the learning outcomes can be achieved, and so our learners can achieve the ultimate outcome – to save lives from suicide. This is alongside Mind Matters exhibiting at the 2023 Autism Show this month, and me sharing my late diagnosis story publicly to the biggest forum I have faced to date. I am, of course, also writing this book. Always something up my sleeve, as such. Such projects run alongside the daily operation that is delivering our training, and the infrastructure that supports and surrounds this. We are currently near full capacity, and for reasons I will discuss in the self-care chapter, I do not wish to exceed that capacity, or to grow the business much further. Rarely, if ever, do you hear that from a small business owner, but for me it is essential. It was different in our early years, every effort then was to deliver excellence and grow the business, and where there was space, it would be filled with a project or endeavour that would achieve that goal.

ALL IDEAS ARE BORNE INSIDE OUR HEADS

One such project was 'Hug-in-a-Box©', an idea and product I developed in year one of the business. Hug-in-a-Box© can be described through the following brief I put together at the time.

Hug-in-a-Box©

There are times in all our lives when difficulties and challenges cause us to have a low mood, reduced positivity and increased sadness. Our mood is affected by a variety of things, including issues around us, within us, and a whole host of other direct and indirect causes. For 450 million people worldwide, the cause is mental ill health (World Health Organisation, 2011).

When friends, family and loved ones are experiencing a low mood and sadness, we want to make them feel better, whether that's due to mental ill health, or another difficulty they are currently experiencing. In most, if not all cases, we can't solve their problems, but we still feel the urge to make a positive difference to how they feel.

Improving how someone feels in a positive way can often be done by small things. For example, making someone a drink and offering a non-judgemental listening ear, or helping them get the appropriate professional support they require. On occasion, we must assist or encourage from a distance due to limitations such as geographical location, or other practical restriction, but unanimously we want to help.

Our Hug-in-a-Box© allows you to make a small difference to improve someone's day, wherever their location to you. You can show that you care, want to help and want to make them feel better by sending them a 'Hug'.

The products within Hug-in-a-Box© can help to provide 'perfect moments' – those priceless moments when we feel present, content and able to acknowledge notable happiness within our day.

The contents of Hug-in-a-Box© may vary but will always include:

- Little Book of Mindfulness: *An easy way to gently let go of stress and be in the moment. This little book is something your hug receiver can take with them every day, providing simple 5–10-minute daily exercises to improve mindfulness.*
- Relaxing candle: *The calming effect of candlelight can be a simple yet valued tool to help reduce stress and increase self-awareness. Benefits are further increased by selected scented candles, or merely by scent preference.*

- Camomile tea: *Camomile is historically known for its calming properties. It is extremely effective at helping with anxiety and insomnia – a common symptom associated with depression.*
- Relaxing gel eye mask: *The challenges of modern life can be sources of discomfort and pain, including migraines, eye strain, muscle tension and illness. The relaxing gel eye mask can ease the pressure and pain of these problems, by heating or cooling the product to suit the problem.*
- Dark chocolate: *Mental health benefits include the ability to boost brain levels of endorphins (natural opiates) as well as serotonin (a mood-altering chemical on which many antidepressants act).*
- Relaxing bath salts: *These relaxing bath salts can balance the emotions and help to combat mental fatigue.*

Get Support Now: Helping for the long-term

We fully appreciate that our Hug-in-a-Box© won't solve everyone's problems or difficulties. Rather its aim is to provide some 'perfect moments' of respite and recharge that will assist in coping with these problems in a healthy way, or by improving the mood through relaxation.

For many people, however, the greater need may be for the type of support that will create a longer lasting difference. This may include talking therapies, access to trained professionals who can assist with specific issues, or other types of professional support. What we truly hope is that Hug-in-a-Box© becomes the start of a recovery journey.

To increase the likelihood of this being so, we've added a 'Get Support Now' card to Hug-in-a-Box©. Get Support Now allows the hug receiver to find out about (via QR code scanner or by directly accessing the webpage) a wide range of services that can assist with their problem and/or mental ill health. Many of the support services offer 24/7 access to helplines, and other assistance.

Start someone's recovery journey today by giving them a Hug-in-a-Box©.

As the business started to grow in terms of training demand, so too did the orders for Hug-in-a-Box© and they started to become more difficult to administer and distribute. This was the point when I paused and asked myself which would offer the greatest social return on investment and which did I love doing most? The answer was the training, by far. So, we chose to disable the ordering system and stop dispatching Hug-in-a-Box©, in favour of training and meeting the training demand.

In March 2020, the world went into lockdown, a time when I naturally revisited the return on investment of Hug-in-a-Box©, which during lockdown was higher than the training. To this day, I *know* we could have re-engaged something that would have reached high demand during this time. It bridged the distance for loved ones who could not be together. It would have been the perfect way to send a virtual hug and let others know they cared, plus it signposted to lots of mental health related support, which was much needed at the time. This was the real beauty of Hug-in-a-Box©, as it connected people to mental health support in a stigma-free way. It took the shame out of getting mental health support and allowed others to encourage it in a safe and gentle way. This was, in fact, its primary purpose, coveted through a gift. It fitted perfectly with our values and my desire to reduce suffering in others, and now the timing was optimal – Covid lockdown. Did I choose to revive Hug-in-a-Box©? No, the answer is no. Why? Because I was already totally and utterly burned-out, and it took the lockdown, and stepping away from Mind Matters, to show me that. Lockdown and my work disappearing for five months gave me the much needed time to step aside from it all, and to see how it was having an impact on my own mental health. The demand for training pre-Covid – which had outstripped the capacity to distribute Hug-in-a-Box© – had become overwhelming. I just couldn't see it until everything stopped. A lot of lives were lost during Covid, but a lot of lives were saved, too, perhaps my own included.

Pre-Covid, the training had all been developed for face-to-face delivery only, and consequently all our courses were cancelled from the second week of March onwards and did not resume until the licensors developed online versions for instructors to deliver. Timescales on this were out of my control. It took the licensors a few months, and they did a fantastic job of it in a short space of time. I knew they would, and I knew they would do it quickly, as they too would not want their businesses to disappear any more than I wanted my own to, so I relied on that knowing for my own peace of mind, and it paid off. Their time gave me time to rest. The courses were ready by the summer of 2020. I was then required to upskill in the online version and learn how to deliver training online, at which point we were good to go… unless you consider the fact that I struggle incredibly with change and cognitive overload!

As an Autistic trainer, it took me longer than other trainers to adjust, particularly having to manage software functions as well as delivery, but I made optimal use of those around me who *were* able to adjust more quickly than myself – my associate trainer pool, which had been built prior to Covid. I simply hovered in the background working on the infrastructure until I built the confidence and know-how to deliver online myself. My first online course was January 2021, six months after everyone else, and we had an incredibly busy year that year, with significant growth. We were delivering about 98% of our courses online, with the odd face-to-face delivery in the summer months of 2021. Had we pushed Hug-in-a-Box© during lockdown, it may well have compromised our primary purpose when the training demand *did* return. Hug-in-a-Box© was a great product that, should we have wanted to, would have been in high demand, and hopefully would have helped lots of people, but I simply chose not to pursue it further.

At the time, Hug-in-a-Box© was pretty much one of a kind. A rudimentary online search today will show you just how popular the concept became. There are pages and pages of similar products – which is great – and we may well have drowned in the noise in the longer term. The risk then might have been not being able to regain the traction we had with the training. I have no regrets; it was the right business decision, and the right decision for my health.

A few years after Hug-in-a-Box©, I came up with another idea – a system to assist providers to access trainers and trainers to access providers. This idea was borne of one comment, a trainer at a networking event asserting, "I am hanging on to my qualification by its coat-tails," and the suffering he was feeling that I was now feeling too! I will talk more about the impact of being highly empathic and sensitive in chapter ten. The reason the guy said this was that, as training instructors, we need to deliver a set number of courses to maintain our instructor status and qualification to deliver. For this to happen, it requires us to be able to find and reach our market, and to deliver. I knew there were providers who needed excellent trainers, and excellent trainers who needed providers to offer their services to, they just weren't connecting. So, I had worked out a membership system that would redress the disconnect and link the two together. I called it Training Link©. I floated it to key people and providers just before

Covid, but it never took hold – the will, understanding, and in some cases the listening, was not there, and my time was in high demand elsewhere, so I let it go.

When I am in a group where others have their own agenda and are unwilling to listen, even when I know something has potential, I lose interest, fast. My lack of assertiveness, especially in groups, and my lack of time capacity led me to retract. It had been an idea to help others, other trainers and training providers, and to assist Mind Matters as a provider too, but I learned from this that sometimes you just must let others help themselves.

When I come up with such ideas, I am in my most creative state of thinking. There is usually a problem, someone or something has pulled on my heartstrings, and that is what gives me the motivation to seek a solution. Autistics often value fairness and equality and are not comfortable with injustice. We are drawn to correcting issues such as that above. It's a bit like three people in a pub becoming passionate about something and before you know it you have the makings of a small grassroots non-profit organisation existing to resolve an issue for the greater good. When my brain is at its most creative, coming up with ideas and solutions to redress the balance, it is most often in the alpha state.

The alpha state refers to brainwaves that are in alpha flow, or 'the flow', which measure between 8 and 12Hz, as opposed to beta waves, which measure between 12 and 30Hz.[31] Visually they look like the ups and downs of a roller coaster, beta waves having more ups and downs, closer together than the alpha waves, for the more hedonistic coaster rider, so to speak. Alpha occurs when the brain is in 'idle' state, which can occur during many activities – when we are relaxed, meditating, or being mindful. Mundane activities can do this; for example, washing the dishes by hand rather than putting them in the dishwasher. It requires very little cognitive input, so the brain can just 'switch off'. My brain goes into the alpha state when I clean my crystal light fittings, or when I go out for a walk in the garden, and most often when I go running. In running, the alpha state is often referred to as 'the flow'. For me, it's the state when I recognise my brain has gone into 'off' mode, but not fully 'off', as I notice something else starts to happen – I become very creative! I suspect it is a switch from my more dominant left brain to my right brain taking over, finally getting its time and space to speak! When I am running, I get my best ideas, I can create my Autistic scripts for public speaking and training, I can solve problems and find creative and innovative solutions to problems. I've been scripting my talk for the Autism Show for the last month and must be at 30+ times now. It gets better the more I script it when I am in 'the flow'. Some believe this is the state that connects us to the spirit world – the other side – and that's when the universe speaks to us. I am one of those believers. So, one of the best things I can do to get the best out of my brain (and respond to the universe) is to go for a run, or to just relax, but I do struggle with the latter. I try. I sit alone quietly, take three long, deep breaths, counting backwards from one hundred, and visualise my happy place – a white wooden cottage on a cliff, with a white picket fence, gingham curtains, steps down to a nearby beach, warm sunshine, no coastal erosion, and as cliché as could be. It's a good way of putting my brain into alpha but running is *by far* the most effective. Since I know it works for me, I wanted to find a way of putting my brain into alpha waves more often, at times when I wasn't running, for example. I read a few blogs, and after reading the NICE (National Institute for Health and Care Excellence) recommendations on alpha-STIM[32] – an electronic device which puts the brain into alpha and which shows great potential for those with anxiety – I invested in my own alpha-stimulating device. The results so far... I found the device uncomfortable, and it seems to create an electrifying feeling in my teeth, the ones in which I have amalgam fillings! Many Autistics experience dental problems, another comorbid; I have a lot of cavities!

I do often wonder just how much the universe and nature want us to keep things simple, daydreaming, for example, rather than trying too hard with newfangled devices for things it already created naturally, and that already work! Maybe, for me, the alpha-stim device reacting with my fillings was a message from the universe to stop trying to reinvent or overcomplicate things – we already have the tools within us, which it provided a long time ago. Go running.

Autistics are, in fact, very good at daydreaming and 'spacing out'. Being in my head is often a much safer space to be in than the world where I live, so I do this a lot, often visualising what I am trying to work out the answers to, and sometimes just to get away, disassociating. Perhaps I do go into alpha more than I realise?

It's plausible that nature intentionally programmed the Autistic brain type to overthink and 'space out', so humanity could benefit from what the Autistic brain type could achieve in that 'other' state? Problem solving and ideas creating, for example. There is enough research to suggest Autistics and the Autistic neurotype has existed since the dawn of mankind and that we continue to do so because there is a need for the Autistic neurotype amongst humanity, for its survival. We bring something to neurodiversity that nature has and always had intended.

CHAPTER 8

Being Organised and Efficient with Working Memory Problems

Many Autistics will talk about the challenges of 'executive dysfunction'. Just as we know that every Autistic person is different – the spiky profile I refer to in my book *The Umbrella Picker* – we know that each Autistic person may have no issues at all with this, some issues with this, or many issues with this, and each to various degrees.

Executive dysfunction refers to our brain's ability to organise, plan, pay attention and our ability to inhibit appropriate responses. It is thought that up to 80% of Autistics experience it.[33] I am no exception, but living undiagnosed and unsupported for a very long time, and with high-level anxiety, I was caused to work much of it out and to create compensatory strategies myself.

My biggest challenge is 'working memory'. Working memory refers to the ability to retain strings of information in the short-term, flit to something else, retain the former information, and return to it at another not-too-distant point. In our household we have a saying: "Once it's gone, it's gone." In most cases, what we would like to remember *must* be written down, or if it is an object, it must be placed within our vision, or anchored. An example would be, I don't easily forget to check my emails, so I email the thing I want to remember to myself; or I rarely forget my bag or car keys, as I usually can't leave without them, so I anchor things to those. I use what I can remember easily, things in my long-term memory, to assist with what I cannot, the things in my short-term memory. Nearly everything must be written down. I either email a reminder there and then – I cannot wait a couple of minutes or it's gone – or I anchor reminders to something else there and then. Where possible, I just do the thing straight away so as not to forget. This comes with a risk that I accidentally do tasks twice, forgetting that I have already done them! Our Autistic son is the same. I can ask Oliver to go and get me the dirty laundry to load into the washing machine, he leaves the room, two minutes later he comes back, totally oblivious. I say, "Did you get me the washing?" "Oh, sorry," and off he goes for the second time. There is no guarantee that it will happen the second time around, but on each forget, the likelihood of remembering increases. For me, it requires patience, something I struggle with, so I work hard to control my impatience, or I go and do it myself. All this is tiresome. If my self-control stocks have been used elsewhere, e.g., social masking all day, I won't have much capacity left for patience, so then I become irritable. We all only have so much control, the more it's expended, the closer to the end of the tether we reach. My tether isn't a short one, but as an Autistic, I expend a lot of self-control on other things. This is highly demanding and outstrips the stocks.

I find in Autistic people there are lots of contradictions. We can be like an enigma to others (and sometimes to ourselves too). We may have poor working memory but will often have superior fact recall, attention to detail, and excellent long-term memories. You can be sure that the thing you forgot easily – good or bad – we haven't, and when we regurgitate it years later, you will be surprised. A few times I have recited something like, "How did your house move go, are you settled in now?" to someone I've met in my line of work only a couple of times (but worked hard to retain the information for future small talk reference) and they've given me a look of surprise that I remembered it. Sometimes it's a look of curiosity, 'she pays attention', then they make extra effort to talk to me in future, and so the small talk goes on, often at my own expense. Small talk is hard for me, I must prepare well in advance for it. In a world where many people don't feel listened to, where people are so easily distracted by technical devices, my ability communicates something positive that is attractive to others – I listened, I heard and I remembered – it communicates someone cared enough. What no one sees is the effort I put behind this, and the reason I do it, which is that I have lived a life feeling unheard and misunderstood and I don't want others to feel the same way. Years ago, I did a bit of work shadowing at a job centre, and one of the workers had a little black book kept in her drawer. She wrote something personal about each and every person she was supporting, so that when they returned to future appointments, she could ask about it. It made her personable and illustrated to them that they mattered. Different strategy, same outcome. Her reason for doing so – she cared – enough to make the effort! This making someone feel they are the most important person in the room is a resilience skill; resilience is an attitude, it's about feeling fabulous and helping others to feel fabulous too. This lady had engineered a great tool so that she too could remember, and she used it to help others to feel good about themselves. My brain will do this if I make a conscious effort and if I anchor it to the person or place. I simply anchored the house move to where the person told me. I go back to that place and it's the first thing I remember when I see them. It can be the name of someone's grandchild or another circumstance. I just work out what gives them a rosy glow and work hard to remember it. I treat the information as facts to be remembered and recognise the positive power of this. Ask me what I went to the fridge for, or what I ate for dinner yesterday, or why I went back upstairs three minutes ago, and you have no chance! I think my brain likes facts and dumps the irrelevant to make space for what it sees as valuable. That's one explanation, I guess.

Sometimes my poor working memory can be used in a favourable way, or in reverse for favourable return. For years, I was very poor at money management, again a common outcome of executive dysfunction and other factors such as impulse control, and made worse if linked to an obsession, because then I am relying on inhibition.

STRENGTH *not* DEFECIT

Many Autistics struggle with impulse control with their Autism. For me, it is the pair of shoes I have seen, or something I really want connected with a collection or an obsession. I use delay tactics as a mechanism to manage this, forcing myself to put some time between me and the item. If I still want it with the same gusto a few hours or days later, then I may give in to the urge. Again, how much control I have will be dictated by lots of factors – stress, how much I have been social masking, or expending control elsewhere. If I am low on control stocks, I am vulnerable to impulsiveness. My most beneficial financial management solution developed when the pain of change became less than the pain of staying the same, and my anxiety around money (or lack of) in my late twenties just became too much *not* to act. Ironically, my poor working memory was the solution.

So, I am bad at remembering, or in reverse, good at forgetting. So, I set up a range of places to store money, so I forget I have it and therefore don't spend it. My good at forgetting brain forgets I have done this, and so I have successfully hidden money from myself. It works to help me save. I don't forget forever! So, from my late twenties, I was able to turn things around, but I still use the same strategy today, and I use it for my business finances also. It also has the advantage of spreading the risk of things like banking fraud. I forget in the short-term but not the long-term. Unfortunately, my daughter also uses my poor working memory to *her* advantage! She borrows £100 from me and knows if I haven't written it down or written when she must return it, I will fail to remember. She keeps quiet about it and hopes I do not remember – free £100! Sometimes I do, sometimes I don't, and she gets lucky. Laura's working memory is poor too, and she has strategies that aid her. One of them is to use me and my strategies to support *her* poor working memory.

Challenges with cognitive flexibility are something I experience, and link with the social masking I also use to survive. Cognitive flexibility allows us to switch between concepts and return to the previous one. I am easily distracted, especially by visual things, and it requires a lot of self and impulse control not to be. Whether it's a person walking by my window when I am working, something colourful or sparkly, which draws me in like a magpie – I once bumped my car into another car staring at someone's Christmas tree through their window(!) – or a person needing my attention. I find all of that incredibly difficult, especially if I am hyper-focused on something else, my work or obsessions, for example. If it is a person who distracts me, straight away I must switch on the social mask. This is cognitive whiplash in and of itself. If I have been distracted, attempting then to re-engage with where I left off can be very difficult, and sometimes impossible, whereas a neurotypical may simply switch back to where they left off more seamlessly.

This cognitive inflexibility means I also struggle with change. I need structure, sameness, a clear plan, and the plan to be maintained. As a very visual Autistic, I work on a visual plan. Many other cognitive processes are linked to

STRENGTH not DEFECIT

the visual picture, so when someone or something changes that, it will feel impossible to cope with. I can also have trouble if I use the wrong visual. When I am scripting for a talk, for example, I sometimes make the mistake of visualising me talking on stage, but that is not the visual I will have on the day, so it totally throws me. I must remember the visual is the audience, not me, otherwise I have given myself an unnecessary visual change to deal with. This will be heightened in a situation where I am working hard at masking and once again using up the control reserves. This would be a time when my social masking is most likely to fracture. I need to be forewarned of change, not told two seconds before, especially when it is something of high importance to me or linked to my obsession. I can often struggle delivering courses with co-trainers if my co-trainer diverts even slightly from a plan we have agreed, which means I generally prefer solo deliveries and courses that can be delivered solo. It will be hard for the other trainer to fully comprehend the impact the change has on me. For this (and a few other reasons) I took the decision this year to remove a course from our portfolio because it was a mandatory co-delivery course.

I think executive dysfunction is one of the reasons why I struggled to learn to drive in my early twenties. It took me a year back in 1997 when I was twenty-one. I found it incredibly difficult, and it's one of the patterns I see in other Autistics. If we do learn to drive, we learn later, not at seventeen like many young people keen to do so as soon as they have their birthday, or if we learned to drive earlier it won't have come easily to us, or we just don't drive at all (like my mum). Was it not for my first husband, I would never have finished my driving lessons; he pushed me to do it, so I persevered. I find the driving ability pattern changes if the person has ADHD with their Autism, or if they just have ADHD. If ADHD is present, it appears to be far less of a challenge from what I can tell. There is something about it that I feel Autistics struggle with, and I suspect it is the cognitive overload, which causes overwhelm, and the lack of control, which ultimately equates to us feeling stressed. We then become too stressed by it, don't make the best decisions, and might even be told off by the driving instructor. I hate being told off or feeling I am in trouble. I passed my driving test first time because I am subservient, took every instruction literally and followed the process and rules to the letter! I drive lots with my job, but it will never be the thing I find easiest. I use two satellite navigation systems, and research journeys and venues before travel for each course. Travelling via public transport is more difficult, however; it's too peopley and exhausts me more than driving my car. Again, I am not saying I can't do it, I'm just saying it's more difficult, and I must work harder than most.

I am a realist. Change can and does happen, interruptions will occur and not *everything* can be predicted. So, for my company to deliver upwards of 160 courses a year, and to a high degree of excellence, it is essential I can find solutions to such challenges.

I work visually and I work with time, to the minute!

STRENGTH *not* DEFECIT

Choose who we are, Autistic or Allistic, wealthy or poor, we all share one very precious commodity – 168 hours in a week, no more, no less. I work backwards from any deadline. If a deadline is set for four weeks' time, I go back to the start and I plan precisely how quickly a task can be out of the way and complete so that I can relax. I have become very adept at knowing exactly how long a task will take. My left-brained precise calculation of time, and the fact that I actually struggle to relax, instead filling the spare time with something else, and performing tasks faster than most, contributes to a higher-than-average productivity level, and, of course, discomfort with any interruptions to my schedule. I am not alone in being a highly productive Autistic. James Mahony, the head of Autism at Work at JPMorgan Chase & Co., says that Autistic employees were "… as much as 140% more productive than their peers."[34]

I simply cannot leave a task till the last minute, unless doing so is *totally* out of my control, in which case I am able to accept that. I have a very clear black and white sphere of control.

I remove as much of the unpredictable as possible. If something is important to me and I know there is potential for disabling stress, e.g., the cognitive overload of driving to a new training venue, finding parking, thinking about what I have to do when I get there, Autistic scripting, etc., and it will make things easier to have a pre-prepared plan A, B and C, then I put those plans in place beforehand. I usually have the plan written on a sticky note on my dashboard where I can see it when I need it. I create the plan when

I am *not* stressed – not when I am stuck in a foreign city centre trying to find parking! If I can predict stress, I can remove or prevent it through effective organisational skills. I recognise what causes me stress and put the plans in place beforehand. I do this because I am not a spontaneous thinker, I need time to think. This is made worse if I am stressed or anxious, so I *plan* for being stressed and my anxiety spiking. I won't *always* be able to circumvent it but often I can. My brain is routinely thinking about steps so far down the line that others won't even comprehend. I have had to learn to do that because I cannot cope otherwise. I am carrying an umbrella on a sunny day.

Training, of course, isn't just about the process of getting you to the room ready to facilitate, it's about the training delivery, the most important part. My executive functioning challenges do not end when I start to speak. If anything, they are amplified. Some of this I simply 'own' as a trainer – call out in front of my learners with humour. Knowing much of what I experience is because I am Autistic helps, I can share that humour too. I am quite a serious person, but can also laugh at myself, unless I am near burnout, at which point I lose my sense of humour. I tell my audience about my 'brain fireworks', the explosion in my brain that happens when I get so impassioned about something that my thoughts go everywhere. I lose my train of thought, and it can take me a few minutes to follow it back. My trains of thought also get derailed – the mind blanks! I own it. I figure that, provided 98% of what I deliver is high quality, including high quality knowledge, the rest

STRENGTH *not* DEFECIT

will be viewed as me being a little quirky and 'different', which of course I am. I disclose I am an Autistic trainer, and because of 'ableism', some will drop their expectations of me at that point anyway, which then becomes a beautiful opportunity to challenge the ableism in the room and open learners' minds to what non-stereotypical Autism looks like, and just how 'able' it can actually be. Our courses aren't about Autism, but I get the opportunity to indirectly teach them about it anyway. It adds another dimension and, in my opinion, 'added value' to what we deliver. My Autism allows me to recall lots of facts, interesting stories and strands of information, which further adds to the learning. I don't think I would do this quite so well if I wasn't Autistic. Hopefully it more than makes up for the brain fireworks or my derailed trains of thought. I can often identify when I have an Autistic learner on a course, as they spot the detail others usually miss. They will question, maybe seem pedantic to others, when they are just seeking to understand and build an accurate picture. Their thinking is often layered in sophisticated ways that sometimes blows my mind. It's a privilege to have them in the room and often enhances the learning for all of us.

Mind Matters delivers anything from three to eight courses a week during term time, dependent on demand. This means my diary can look overloaded – I will have my own course deliveries scheduled, and my associate trainers' deliveries. Mine alone can appear overwhelming visually, so the way I manage this is to break it down. I work two to three weeks ahead, unless it is a bigger project requiring more time, which is planned in as a bespoke timetable. I simply break it down into smaller steps, and some days, I can deal with today and today alone. As I write now, I have a big week ahead of me. Each day has something in it that requires extra planning above what I typically do. If I look at the week ahead as a whole, I will go upstairs (right now) hide under my duvet and surface next week on the other side. For reasons highlighted throughout this book, that is not going to happen, so I simply deal with each bit as it comes, with a cursory glance and reminder of the big picture to keep on target. Never living within your comfort zone means you are more than familiar with discomfort. I am familiar with being out of my comfort zone because I'm never really within it. It's just different types of discomfort I must adapt for.

My central cohesion issues mean I am often looking for the detail, so need to remind myself to look back at the big picture for clarity and understanding. The bigger picture is the pattern and where pattern spotting occurs. I simply home in on the minutiae and join it to a bigger picture, which creates me a pattern or sequence I can theorise from. The most removed picture I struggle with is where the universe ends, and at times it causes me a great existential headache when I try to think about it. I follow a space photography page on social media, and the other day they featured a photograph of a black hole. Scared the hell out of me. Just nothingness through the hole. My brain still hurts from trying to get my head around the image. I take comfort in compartmentalising it as a big unanswered existential question, and why I believe in God.

I have a strong need for order and organisation, maybe because the world can feel so chaotic to me. If I can put a system in place to manage organisation, I will. I am an Autistic who is exceptionally organised, despite the executive functioning issues, because organisation helps me to cope with a lack of predictability in the world. I have routines, and I particularly struggle with visual chaos. I cannot think straight if something is visually 'off', so I must address it first before I can think. Of all my sensory challenges, visual chaos overwhelms me the most and is why my first book was titled *The Umbrella Picker* – a nickname given to me at the age of three by shop assistants in a wool shop I visited with my mum on Saturday afternoons because I picked up all the little bits of paper from the floor, the umbrella-shaped corners of paper bags that had fallen during the week. To this day, I am still compelled to pick detritus up from floors, but I mask it out in public.

> Note: My coping mechanism for disorder is order – effective systems and high-level organisation. This is well received by our clients and stakeholders, they consider our service and business very efficient, and so it contributes to our success.

CHAPTER 9

Social Masking and the Ability to Adapt Quickly

For those who have read my memoir, you will know that a salient feature of my Autistic lived experience is social masking, a strategy I use to survive in a neurotypical world. After my diagnosis, I tried to understand the social masking more and was left feeling that it was something I needed to rid myself of if I was to survive. Other Autistics also told me, "Just stop masking," which turned out to be easier said than done. Today I recognise the reverse is true, my social masking *aids* my survival, and my ability to remove my masks was never just about me. It was about the world out there, and the lack of acceptance that exists within it, yet I can only control my role in the play that is life. The best way to explain my position today is to read this blog I wrote a few months ago, titled 'Why I am unable to stop social masking':

> When people encourage me to be my**self**, *not* to socially mask, or as one Autistic said to me after my diagnosis at the age of forty-five, "Just don't mask!" they make it

totally about me, and totally my responsibility, but it's not just about me, and it never was.

I have socially masked for forty-eight years, and I started masking at the age of four.

What is social masking?

Social masking is mimicking neurotypical behaviour to fit in, or to hide in plain sight, camouflaging. Some Autistics will become very adept at it, to the extent that it plays its own part in them being missed altogether, or late diagnosed, as in my own case. And, we do not have just one 'other' mask, we may well have several. Masking operates at a deep level in my own case. It is so automatic and unconscious that I am known to do it in my dreams. It is now a central feature of the person I am and have become. To some extent, we become the masks we wear, but I also find that our masks are intrinsically linked to our values, so at times, having felt the pressure to wear a mask that does not fit with my values, I will quickly remove myself from the people I am masking for, so I *can* remove it.

What do we mimic?

I have been known to mimic anything and everything; someone's mannerisms, clothing, handwriting, the way they speak (I pick up accents very easily, as do many Autistics), the way someone dances, walks, talks, phrases they use, interests they have, choices (good and bad), anything.

Why do Autistics socially mask?

Social masking is a coping mechanism, a survival strategy. We use it to survive in the community with the rest of the 'social herd'. It helps us to stay alive. However, social masking comes with its own cost... When we have been overloaded with situations where we need to socially mask, we will be totally and utterly exhausted. It is one of the reasons I need a lot of solitude – to decompress from the masking. It takes a great deal of self-control to socially mask, and self-control takes energy, so my tolerance levels for other things can become low, e.g., tolerance for noise, impatience, temperature. If I am forced to switch masks quickly, or I am forced to mask in a situation I wasn't expecting, e.g., I bump into someone in the supermarket, I don't always have the energy to deliver. Having to don a mask quickly has a whiplash effect on me. Ultimately, social masking over a long period of time increases the likelihood of mental illness and suicidality in those who use it as a coping mechanism, not unlike other negative coping mechanisms. It is dangerous.

The motivation for me to start socially masking came about because I recognised my own social deficits early on, and because the tribe (society) quickly showed me that it is was not acceptable or safe to be myself, Autistic. It wasn't safe in 1979 when I was four, and it's still not safe now. Autistics are often viewed as weird and different (in negative ways), criticised, rejected and treated negatively in the forms of bullying, control, coercion, discrimination and other forms of direct and indirect abuse. This can happen even when we *do* socially mask, let alone when we don't. So, if I am to remove my masks and be totally authentic, I need to know it's safe for me to do so, and as I see it, forty-three years on, it is still *not* safe to do so.

I am likely to be able to down-mask when I can believe wholeheartedly that I will be accepted, supported and not rejected for who I really am, and until that day arrives (or I am able to not care about those things) then I don't see how I can simply 'down-mask'. Not only do *I* have to change, but society must change also. If it wants social masking Autistics to down-mask, society needs to make it safe for us to be ourselves. We ask for the same acceptance as other minority groups, e.g., LGBTQ+ and BAME, amongst others (and yes, there is work to be done there too). Most people are much more themselves when they feel safe to *be* themselves. I do often

SOCIAL MASKING AND THE ABILITY TO ADAPT QUICKLY

> wonder if our masking conveniences society so well that society is not motivated to support our change. Why challenge a status quo that serves the majority – neurotypicals?
>
> If someone is hiding their identity or true self, there is a reason for it, and the reason may not just be them.

The reason I share this, as well as to help you the reader understand what Autistic social masking is, is to highlight one of the last points, which is that my social masking serves *others* well. They like it. I recognise this, and I fully recognise that I may not be accepted without it. As I've previously mentioned, it is of course an illusion, but not for me – I know I don't 'fit in'. Rather, it is an illusion for you that serves me as well. It has you thinking I'm high-functioning, you accept me and I am safe. If the benefit didn't outweigh the cost, I would likely have been able to remove it by now. I am comfortable with disclosure, but disclosure isn't just about being able to say, "I am Autistic," it is about feeling safe enough to down the myriad social masks that also hide us. The question I am asking myself constantly is, "Am I safe with you?" If you meet me, I am likely to disclose my Autism quite early on – it's my obsession, remember? – but you will *never* see me consciously unmask in your presence. My masks can 'slip', however. This happens when I am tired, in physical pain (I unmasked once during the birth of my second child), or drunk – so I very rarely drink, and only with those who I can unmask with, and when I am in a situation where I do not need to be in control.

My masks have other benefits. I can flex them to fit a situation, a person, or a group of people, and people tell me I am down to earth and personable. I observe (in detail), I read people, and I switch masks accordingly, and quickly. I sometimes recognise I am doing it, but not always. It is so ingrained. I want to be clear here in saying that I am not talking about switching alters, as in conditions such as dissociative identity disorder, though you can see the risk therein of such a misdiagnosis, I feel, especially since most Autistics have experienced trauma and often display trauma responses, just like those diagnosed with DID. And yes, everyone masks to an extent, most people are aware of that – a social mask, a work mask, a telephone voice mask. Autistic masking is different, it is amplified, and it is about survival in a world that does not accept our authentic Autistic selves. So, I mask because it serves us *both*. It exhausts me and has an impact on me in other ways, but because the benefit still outweighs the cost, I have worked out that I *do not* need to stop masking, I just needed a compromise. That compromise is an agreement with myself to '*strategically* mask'.

Strategic masking is me masking when I need to for survival and to continue a career and business I love, to not be totally alone and rejected by society. I am not self-sufficient, I need other people for my survival, but not so much socially. It's a symbiotic relationship where *I* must adapt so *others* will meet my needs; basic survival, as I see it.

SOCIAL MASKING AND THE ABILITY TO ADAPT QUICKLY

So, my compromise is to mask where and when I need to, for my needs to be met, but permit myself enough downtime and solitude so I can unmask and recuperate when I need to, also for my survival. Masking is a contradiction – it's used for survival, but it is dangerous and risks our Autistic lives too, so you have to be flexible with it. Ability to mask and flexibly mask may well be variables which influence Autistic life expectancy, which sadly isn't great either.

Let me do a little test of *your* acceptance. I am a professional trainer, online and face-to-face. I am taken seriously, and people respect me, my knowledge, my ability and my business. I have my trainer mask on and fulfil the role of a competent trainer. I'm easy for you to accept.

Let's instead imagine that I am delivering a training course to you and your colleagues, maybe on the subject matter of suicide prevention, and suddenly I start to display self-stimulating behaviour or Autistic stimming, maybe some hand flapping, or I start decluttering the room and straightening things up while I am delivering your course, so I can calm myself and think more effectively, or during the break I sit down and start vocal stimming. What if I start to emotionally dysregulate during a film because my empathy connects at such a level with the content or story that I cry? What if I've not cried for a while, and can't stop crying, those tears fuelled by the preceding weeks of trying to survive as an Autistic? Are you still accepting me now? Are you still taking me seriously? Are you still respecting me as your trainer? Are you embarrassed by my behaviour? Will you later comment about me using words like 'strange', 'weird', or, "I'm not sure that this person should be a trainer. I can't believe they cried!" Now, of course I am not suggesting everyone would think like this, but I am inclined to think *many* would, and I think I would lose training bookings very quickly. My unmasked Autistic self can be very irritable, moody, have a desperate need to order, directness in how I speak, perceived as pedantic, and I just don't think that would bode very well in the training room. So, essentially, I believe I have two options: 1) Mask and buy into the social contract and expectations of the world as it happens to be currently, to **survive**; or 2) Unmask and prepare myself for my world to change dramatically – loneliness, unemployment, loss of purpose, isolation – **risk of ill health and the reduced life expectancy that coincides** – I don't think I would survive. I think I would lose many friends and contacts who are happy to accept my masked Autistic self but may be far less willing to accept my true Autistic self. I think I'd be left only with those who love me unconditionally, which isn't very many. Anyone else doesn't love me enough to accept my Autistic self. This I see in an Autistic family member, who hasn't been accepted for being her true self, and from whom family and friends have removed themselves. It is easy to verbally disclose, "I am Autistic," but true disclosure will be the day I can down-mask fully everywhere and with everyone. If I am expecting that kind of change in the near future, I may be very disappointed. It's all about survival, for all of us, but I have to work much harder for it to happen.

So instead, I think very carefully about what I want to say,

SOCIAL MASKING AND THE ABILITY TO ADAPT QUICKLY

censor what I say and how I say it, play down my obsessions, and many other things that facilitate the illusion for you of your 'normal'. Keep in mind also that my obsessions are of a nature that they are socially acceptable and culturally blend in, unless of course I talk too much about them to the point I see someone's eyes glaze over. This is my weak spot. I can see when this happens, it's subtle, but doesn't go unnoticed. I don't read facial expressions so well, but I'm good at reading eyes. This is the reason I like cameras 'on' when I'm delivering training; I read eyes, although it is easier when I am delivering face-to-face than online. I didn't aim for my obsessions to be socially acceptable ones, that's just how it worked out, electric pylons notwithstanding! I am obsessed with mental health (not out of the ordinary in today's world), running (overall thought of quite favourably, but I have been nicknamed Forrest Gump by some!), reading (associated positively with learning and intelligence by neurotypical standards), my home and garden (many invest wholeheartedly in these), and the others are mostly in my head, you wouldn't know about them unless I share them with you. My obsessions aren't train timetables (very stereotypical, and I apologise for that), and had the electric pylons have developed into full-blown obsession (I don't have control over this), I would have hidden it as much as possible. I am so well practised at social masking, I can do it with ease, and perhaps more effectively than most neurotypicals, who will of course mask at times – which will be exhausting for them too – and may not be executed so easily. I've masked so much and for so long I even mask in my dreams. I can wake up knowing I was masking within an interaction in the dream.

Because I mask so well, it is often mistakenly assumed that I am a so-called 'high-functioning' Autistic. My views on high and low-functioning labels are highlighted in my memoir, but suffice to say, I am neither and yet I am both. Society likes to label my functioning as a measure of how well I fit into *their* world. High-functioning was created by neurotypicals, not by Autistics: "This one fits in well, makes it easy for us" – accept – "This one is low-functioning, makes it difficult for us" – reject. And the truth? Only an Autistic person can tell you how well they believe they are functioning at any given time – mentally and physically – and how much they are masking to hide the truth. My ability to function changes constantly, it is my masks that are more consistent, hence why I say I am neither yet both. It's just another example of something made by others for us, not with us.

CHAPTER 10

People Pleasing and the Empathy Advantage

"My name is Jane McNeice, and I am a 'people pleaser' in recovery" … who does not want to lose her empathy in the process!

I have for a long time known I am a highly sensitive person, or HSP, and that I am an empath, an HSP-empath, if you will. I think these are beautiful qualities, I wouldn't want to change them, but I would often like to reduce the pain and challenge they cause. They carry risk, a greater risk of Autistic burnout, and a greater statistical risk of developing conditions like depression. I feel the weight of them when I am around others, particularly when others are in pain – mental, physical, or both.

Many Autistics are HSPs and empaths. This may surprise you if you have bought into the stereotypical myth that Autistics do not have empathy, that they are hypo-empathic. It is just *that*, a myth. I explain in my memoir *The Umbrella Picker* that we process empathy differently, that is all. I also highlight in there the 'double empathy problem'.[35] I actually believe there is a lot of hidden Autism in HSP-empaths.

STRENGTH *not* DEFECIT

The stereotype is often of the Autistic who works in STEM – science, tech, engineering, and maths – and yes, that is likely where you will find those Autistics with the kind of profile or personality that is suited to STEM, maybe a more stereotypical Autistic, someone with what Simon Baron-Cohen describes in his book *The Pattern Seekers*, a more systemising or super-systemising brain,[36] but I firmly believe there are also a lot of non-stereotypical Autistics, the empaths and super-empaths, who are instead working in the 'helping' industries. They are just that, the 'helpers' of the world. We are drawn to health and social care careers, causes, putting right social injustice, jobs involving feelings such as those in mental health and the psychological sciences, and spiritual vocations. Our mission is simple, to ease the pain of others as much as possible. Why? Because we feel it too. You cry, I taste your tears. I really do. It can be fuelled further if the Autistic is obsessed with 'people', and their fascination or interest has led to a career in 'helping' people because of what they have learned about them, through intense 'people watching', for example.

Autistics, I find, are a group of people less scared of what some might regard as the darker manifestations of human pain, e.g., self-harm, substance misuse, crime, or illnesses that are stigmatised by many such as eating disorders, psychosis, etc. I think that Autistic people are less likely to pathologise them, and more likely to view them as just different ways of coping and being unwell. This may well be the case because many Autistics have in fact experienced these issues themselves, they've been the 'person in need', the person with an eating disorder or who has self-harmed to cope. Many who have experienced them and sought treatment will often talk about that *one* professional, a 'helper', who *totally* understood them, the one who 'got it'. Could it be the case that the one who 'got it', the helper they 'connected' with, did so because they shared the same neurotype?

Most Autistics will tell you they feel misunderstood by most other people, but not other neurodivergents, especially other Autistics. Are the 'helpers' who understand us some of the other undiagnosed (and in some cases diagnosed) Autistics, who are high on the empath scale, maybe what Simon Baron-Cohen describes as the 'super-empaths'?[37]

Autism, I believe, is highly prevalent in my industry, the 'helping industries', but of a non-stereotypical Autistic type that is more empath and super-empath than systemiser, the highly sensitive type of Autistic rather than the systemiser-brained types who you will more likely find in STEM. I'm asking you to be open-minded and not to subscribe to the myth and stereotype that Autistics lack empathy, otherwise the empath Autistic will continue to be overlooked. Autistics in STEM are not faced with a stereotype that hides them, but rather one that helps to find them. For many of us, our empathy is our 'superpower', though like me, if this is you, you will also be aware that it comes at a cost. It can have a negative impact on our health, make us vulnerable, and is one of the key drivers for 'people pleasing'.

My people pleasing is borne out of the fact that I can feel your pain, very often your emotional pain. When

STRENGTH *not* DEFECIT

I feel your pain, it is desperately uncomfortable and at times can quite literally overwhelm me. Because of this, I am motivated to reduce it. It's unpleasant for you, and therefore unpleasant for me too. I feel your emotions as if they are my own, so to reduce our mutual discomfort I am going to attempt to rid you of your pain. One of the ways I will attempt to do this is to quickly look for a solution for your problem or need, or please you in some way. So, what does that look like? People pleasing.

People pleasing can be trying to do things for you that make you happier, meeting a need quickly, or dismissing my own needs in favour of yours, and more subtly, agreeableness, toning down my views on an issue, wanting to fix and offer solutions when I am instead trying to empower you to do that for yourself. It looks like trying to make you happy. I can pick up on your mood within moments of being in your presence because I can feel it. If you are frightened, I want to reassure. If you are upset, I want to dry your tears. I want to take away your pain because it is now my pain too. We are in it together.

Empathy is a high standard – a standard of love – over and above sympathy and pity, a love that starts with us, but when you are a people pleaser, that feeling is being sought elsewhere rather than in yourself first. It is hard to learn to love yourself when you have lived with the low self-esteem common in many late diagnosed Autistics. It comes from being lost for a very long time, and only when you are found can you start to build self-worth and learn to love yourself first.

PEOPLE PLEASING AND THE EMPATHY ADVANTAGE

Many people have to work at finding the empathy connection, and for others it just happens. For an Autistic who is an empath or super-empath, feeling *all* the time, it can be totally overwhelming. It can be debilitating. As I write, I wonder how many of the NHS professionals currently leaving the industry because of compassion fatigue and burnout are these hidden Autistics who have simply reached the end of the road.

I worked out more recently that my ability to become a *recovered* people pleaser will come down to whether I can get comfortable with other people's (and therefore my own) unpleasant emotions. If the person is angry or irritable, resisting the urge to ease their anger or irritability. Given a lifetime of anxiety, you'd think I *would* be comfortable, but I am not. My life is centred around trying to manage it out and avoiding conflict so as not to upset others and therefore myself. I then question, do I *want* to be fully recovered, or do I just need a better balance of not having to please everyone all the time? The same flexibility I apply to social masking.

In my field of work, I encounter at least one person each week displaying Autistic traits, sometimes obvious signs of Autism (which, of course, can only be qualified by a diagnostician able to test for Autism, not by me). I hear their managers saying things like, "My team struggle to regulate their emotions." Well, they would, but you need their gift – their gift is their empathy – they are good at what they do *because* they are empaths, but they might also struggle to regulate their emotions *because* they are empaths.

STRENGTH *not* DEFECIT

They come as one. You'll need to support the dysregulation in the way(s) the person needs it when they need it. I never refer to thinking someone is Autistic, the focus in the room is the issue, not their neurotype. Instead, the discussion might centre around self-care and the self-care needs that are required if you are an empath.

I try very hard not to always assume Autism, to be mindful of my frame of reference, and I am most definitely not qualified to diagnose it. But as a pattern spotting empathic Autistic, I will pick up on patterns and feelings very quickly, and I am hyper-alert to Autism. I don't get to switch that 'off' for yours or my own convenience, it doesn't have an 'off' switch. They are qualities I have which, I believe, are linked to the fact that I am Autistic, and I can't un-Autistic myself just because it's inconvenient to certain others, e.g., clinical professionals, that I can pattern spot other Autistics (but I can and do censor what I say to others). Both the pattern spotting and empathy have played a part in the success of my business.

The patterns are obvious to me, I see them visually, and they are webbed. I average one in eleven people where I see Autistic traits, or where someone recognises themself from my story and a connection is made. I know the latter because when I share my 'lived experience', people come back and tell me it resonates, and they 'connected' with it. They start to become very questioning, asking me details. They too think they could be Autistic; they self-identify. Some later come back and tell me they are now diagnosed Autistic. The courses we deliver at Mind

Matters attract the helpers, the empaths and the highly sensitive, and those who may appear 'different' or who may be considered outliers, of which I am one. Perhaps this means there is a greater likelihood an unidentified autistic will be amongst my learners? My business gives me a window to the non-stereotypical Autistics who are high on the empath scale, and the super-empaths. I spot the more stereotypical Autistics if I am delivering in STEM or to those working in STEM. Predominantly the non-stereotypical Autistics will be women, women who are more likely to be socially masking Autistics, and where the greatest gap exists between known diagnosed Autistics and actually Autistic.

I believe this group is hidden because Autistics who are empaths and super-empaths are more likely to socially mask than those who are systemiser or super-systemiser types, another reason the systemisers typically get identified younger where the empaths are so often missed. Or maybe they mask less *because* they were identified earlier. Why would an empath mask more? Because the highly empathic are not just seeing, but *feeling* your disdain towards us when we unmask, so we remain masked not to upset you, and therefore not to upset us. I frequently hear unpleasant comments about unmasked Autistics. As an aside, I believe an unmasked Autistic is more likely to be diagnosed with a personality disorder such as BPD/EUPD than a masked Autistic, another group I've also heard unpleasant comments about. Have BPD/EUPD inadvertently become the distinguishing tool for masked or unmasked Autistic,

STRENGTH *not* DEFECIT

I wonder? This too reminds me to keep masking for my own safety.

Super-empaths are hyper-sensitive to your feelings. We do it for you, and for us. I am terribly uncomfortable if I accidentally do or say something in an unmasked, unfiltered way, especially if I think this has upset you. Your body language, or something you say or don't say, tells me about your dissatisfaction with my unmasked self. I'm traumatised by it, because you can be sure I won't ever forget that moment and the emotional memory that goes with it. Autistics are much more easily traumatised than Allistics. We carry lots of little 't' traumas, which mount up, and sadly for many of us, a big 'T' trauma or two as well. If I wasn't so desperately uncomfortable, I'd have dropped the masking a long time ago. This is just another reason I continue to mask, and again, it still speaks of safety and survival, and why so many of us empaths might be hidden.

I also anticipate that the higher we go up the age groups, the graph would go up in terms of just how many are hidden, versus those diagnosed. If I am delivering training in engineering, I will see traits in some of the engineers, the systemiser brain type Autistics, and sometimes signs of ADHD and other neurodivergent conditions. Like myself, they are often very black and white thinkers, at face value may appear less empathic, yet still they have found themselves in my training room wanting to train as a 'helper', so I know this isn't the full picture of them. If they had no empathy, they wouldn't volunteer for such a role. They might even express that they want to become more empathic because someone told them they weren't, and it bothers them enough to be in the room. Perhaps because their brains *are* more systemiser based, what you gain at one end of the scale, you appear to lose at the other? I say appear because I think it's more a processing issue rather than a loss of empathy per se. Though I am an empath, I still show the systemiser qualities you might expect in a pattern spotting Autistic. They are not mutually exclusive. On test, I pattern spot 87% faster than my neurotypical counterparts, but I still have high levels of empathy, it's just that I can be slower than others to show it because I am still processing the cognitive side of empathy. Maybe our slower cognitive processing of painful emotions helps Autistics to manage them, so we don't become too overwhelmed too quickly? Maybe it was inbuilt to help us.

I'm concerned that the over focusing, narrow assumptions and cultural stereotypes of the nerdy Autistic, such as *The Big Bang Theory*'s Sheldon Cooper character (and other media depictions of predominantly male Autistics) misleads people to think Autism is most present in men, or that we all want to be data analysts, software developers, threat detectors, or to work in science, maths, engineering, or tech, and this is leaving us blind to other industries who need our skills, and where you will more than likely find us already working. I see the stereotype whenever I see a job vacancy from an organisation supporting Autistics into work or employment. The job will almost always be centred around computer programming or systemising of some kind. I assure you that you would *not* want me

STRENGTH *not* DEFECIT

programming your software, and most definitely not building your hardware! Quite frankly, for someone who can meet the social requirements of my industry, though admittedly must work harder than most, I find such job adverts blinkered and insulting to me as an Autistic. This behaviour continues to be driven by stereotypical assumptions of where Autistics are best placed vocationally, which will benefit some Autistics – the systemisers – but perhaps not others like me. Job opportunities like that are not representative of *all* Autistics, but rather reflective of the types of Autistics who got found and are therefore more known about, and our failure to find the non-stereotypical Autistics is fuelling the stereotype further. We need to break this cycle if things are to change.

On a personal level, I find this disheartening because it tells me I am still an 'outlier' even in my own community and will remain so until the other non-stereotypical Autistics like me are found. This would be one of my less altruistic reasons to find others – I still feel alone.

I went to an Autism Show recently. I still felt like an 'outlier' there too, despite its commendable attempts to be a supportive environment for Autistic people. Why? Because the stereotype was still more visible than not. My outlying stood out when I spoke to other people, particularly other exhibitors, their demeanour towards me shifting the moment I disclosed, but up to that point no recognition and treated simply like another exhibitor, another professional. Their treatment of me shifted quickly from treating me as a 'professional' to treating me as a 'service user' or 'customer' the moment I disclosed. What changed, I wonder, when I shared I was Autistic? What were they now thinking, or starting to think? What I witnessed was the moving in of 'ableism' now standing between us, but I could also see the curious working out what they had missed about me that they weren't so familiar with, but maybe should be. Many exhibitors would be highly exposed to Autistic people and have high knowledge of Autism, but were they exposed to non-stereotypical Autism, I wonder? I felt I had moved a few notches down in their expectations of me. I don't want this to sound like paranoia, I am simply illustrating what I observed and that I can spot an acute level of detail in other people – the said, the unsaid, mannerisms, eye movement, body language – details many people will miss, and I am sentient.

My pattern seeking serves me well, but at times tells me things I don't want to know, as well as things that I do. It benefits me as an entrepreneur and a business owner, where I can spot changing trends earlier than most, and my masking and ability to please people means I can meet many of my client and learner needs quickly. I work very well in the 'helping industries', though continue to live with a pervasive sense of not being 'good enough' and 'falling short of the mark' in some way. I often feel like a child in an adult's body who is fraudulently tricking others that I am successful. This narrative is common in women who have lived undiagnosed autistic for most of their life – the so-called 'Lost Girls'[38] – but for me is improving since my diagnosis, though only slowly as my self-esteem improves. I have forty-five years to put right, so it was never going to happen overnight. Because of this narrative, I have to drop my measures to 'good enough', rather than 'perfection', and take my measures from objective things in my business that tell me if I am doing okay: my learners and delegates say I deliver excellence based on my course feedback, my clients say they've turned down offerings of free services similar to my own in favour of paying for me and my own company's provision of training and my clients share positive 'word of mouth' commentary, which has been key to our continued and sustainable growth since start-up. Clients return and want to work with us, and our income has grown year on year since start-up. People buy me and my company's service in a very social industry where high social demands are required, and I *can* meet those demands. More importantly, I am not alone as an Autistic in being able to do this. I was hidden for a long time *not* because I couldn't do this, but rather because I *could*. Ableism simply gets in the way of finding people presumed too capable, or too successful to be Autistic because Autistic people are still expected to be disabled. We don't expect Autistics to be successfully working in industries with high social demands, but they are already there, I assure you, which goes back to my earlier point that there are far more Autistics in gainful employment than the research currently illustrates.

The focus on STEM jobs for Autistics illustrates where we might find the more stereotypically Autistic people, the ones who got found, and were often diagnosed in childhood.

Where would I go? STEM? If I was an out of work Autistic, what job are you creating for me to support me back into work? I believe if we were to find *all* the Autistics, we would recognise very quickly that not all of us would be suited to STEM and the very real need for a wider variety of jobs made available for Autistics. As more Autistics do become found, changes like this will, I believe, happen. Otherwise, you will force us into STEM, and we would continue to be the square pegs squashed into round holes that has been the story of our lives, and the gainful employment would not be sustainable. No obsession would form. Some of our profiles (and obsessions) are much better placed in the 'helping' industries. The outdated stereotypes that we cannot 'people' – socially interact, feel, help – are just that, outdated. I would advocate that we are much better placed than many other neurotypes to do work in the 'helping' industries. We've often been on the receiving end, we feel at high levels, and we will passionately want to support and bring about social justice. Our greatest risk will be ourselves – not giving ourselves the due self-care that will be needed when we are successful in this work. We will give it our all, and we will often be good at it *because* of our neurotype and high empathy, but our greatest risk will be burnout because of how much we give.

Not everyone who crosses our path at Mind Matters chooses to work with us, but regardless of whether they purchase some or none of our services, I try to leave people better than I found them. Sometimes an interested party doesn't become our client because they choose to go

STRENGTH *not* DEFECIT

elsewhere for the service they require. This could come down to 'best fit', price, buying local, or another factor. I always wish all prospective clients the best with their well-being plans – it is genuine, and I hope it is received this way. I always highlight we are happy to assist later if they need us, or if their needs change and we can suddenly meet what they require. I want them to feel good, regardless of whether they become our client, or not, and I don't want them to fear coming back to us if it doesn't work out elsewhere. I want us to feel welcoming each and every time someone approaches us. This too is driven by people pleasing, but serves both of us well, and many do take up the invite and return.

I love my vocation, I'm passionate about it, 'good enough' at doing it, and the world most definitely needs it, in particular my community, the Autistic community. *This* is my definition of success. Others may measure my success by my lifestyle, my home, or by my company accounts, but I measure my success by how much I make a difference to the world, which is driven by my values and the empathy which I believe is a key feature and benefit of my Autistic brain type.

CHAPTER 11

No One Way of Communicating

Human beings communicate in a myriad of ways, some easier to understand than others, some viewed as acceptable, and some less so. We may also regress to the path of least resistance, or perhaps the communication method that gets heard or achieves a connection. When it comes to communication, this may not be the path others prefer, but rather the path we prefer, or the path which is fastest and/or safest.

My most comfortable mode of communication has always been writing. I couldn't see that for a very long time, but with hindsight, I can reflect that I have been much better able to express myself and my feelings through the written word than the spoken. I am also more willing to express things in the written word that I wouldn't say in the spoken word. Writing affords me a place to empty out the constant noise in my head, a way to calm, and I am often hyper-focused when I am doing it. I also view it as a creative outlet, the more creativeness I can use in my writing, the more fulfilled I feel. If writing is not your preferred mode of communication, or something you find easy, it can instead cause feelings of frustration, and you are therefore more likely to find an easier path of expressing, which for you might be verbal, or music, or art.

When I have a verbal interaction, I must concentrate on a lot of information to process it quickly, and to respond accordingly in a way that meets the societal 'gold standard', which was decided for me by the predominant neurotype – neurotypicals – not by me. I have two competing issues in any verbal interaction: 1) the social cues and all the information this is delivering, including constant self-checking that I am 'getting it right', and 2) what we are conversing about. I am often overloaded, I shut my eyes to think, shutting out at least one of the other sensory inputs, so as to reduce some of the stimuli that is going in at once. This lack of a sensory filter means the world can feel incredibly chaotic for me. To fit with neurotypical preferences, and for my survival, I also add to this overload with my social masking, and as I've explained, this too is exhausting. Verbal communication does not offer me an easy path, so my preferred way of communicating is through the written word.

Writing allows me to focus on one thing, what I want to say, without the social burden, and to communicate what I want to say today, for others to receive it at a different time, and therefore it does not require the other person to be with me at the same time. It doesn't involve the one-to-one table tennis style interaction that would otherwise cause me added challenges and difficulty. Please be reminded this is not me saying I do not like people, nor am I saying

NO ONE WAY OF COMMUNICATING

I cannot verbally communicate when it's required, I am simply saying verbal communication is not the easiest for me. I am totally fascinated by people and have devoted my life to reducing their pain, but at the same time I must survive, and reducing my pain and stress includes using what is easiest where and when I can. I am no different to anyone else in that respect, as we all do things that help us to navigate and to survive.

Autistic people will show preferences for lots of different ways of communicating, some deemed socially acceptable, and others not. What is acceptable will not be defined by us, but instead by the predominant neurotype, who rarely understand us. Because of this, some Autistics will be shunned and labelled with stigmatising language, e.g. attention-seeking, compounding their sense of isolation and loneliness, or causing them to isolate away from people. Some Autistics will use self-stimulating behaviours, otherwise referred to as stimming or stims to help them to remain calmer. My stims are the swings in my garden or at the park, spinning as a child, and today I stim by spinning my wedding ring on my finger as a calming aid. In the training room, I use Blu-Tack. It helps me to feel less anxious in anxious situations, often situations involving people.

You will see evidence of preferred modes of communication and hidden neurodivergence in the arts, as they afford a different way of communicating for Autistics – music, sculpture, dance and other creative outlets. Such modes of communication offer a method of expressing how we feel when we might not be able to do so otherwise because the societally preferred mode of communication – speaking – is not *our* easiest or preferred method. Keep in mind, also, that some Autistics will be non-verbal all the time, but they may be excellent writers, using instead an alternative mode of communication. Not speaking does not mean having nothing to say. For each of us, whatever communication method is dominant, we tend to become exceptionally good at it. Interesting when Autistic children are viewed as the child who is 'acting out' – nope, not attention seeking – connection seeking, and they too will become *very* good at it! We seek to connect in more ways than people realise.

Of all modes of communication, writing comes easiest to me, but I must remember that reading or writing may not be the preferred mode of others, or I may not know their preferred mode. This I need to consider when writing emails and texts, not to make them too lengthy, which is easier said than done for me. For the spoken part of my business, I must simply work harder than others might need to. One of the tools I use to my advantage is Autistic scripting, and because I am well practised at it, I can make it work in my favour.

Autistic scripting is, in fact, part of social masking, but I have chosen to focus on it as part of communication, as I also see it as a communication style and strategy. Autistic scripting is where an Autistic memorises strings and sequences of dialogue and reuses them as required. Yes, accepted, that's what all people do, and in school you may have done comprehension and missing word tests, which illustrate that there is an expected sequence in most sentences. But with Autistic scripting, we are talking about something much more sophisticated and demanding, highly memorised, and which is delivered just as if it is spontaneous and comes as naturally as breathing to the speaker. It is neither!

A current example of my Autistic scripting is I have a public speaking engagement to do on the 12th of September, a women's business network meeting, where I will be speaking about my lived experience and my business. I started preparing for this talk on the 12th of July, formulating my Autistic script. It's a speaking engagement delivered to a relatively small group, which might seem insignificant to others, but for me it is important because, each time I share my story, it has the power to connect, to find others who were misled into thinking they were neurotypical when they might not be. This is what makes it significant, and as you may recall, *this* is my measure of success.

Some would say, "What's to script? It's not like you don't know your own story." That is true, but for me to speak it with eloquence, clarity and succinctly, which I don't do easily, and to fit it within the time frame of forty minutes that I have been allocated, I need to have a very well-rehearsed script. My script and plan look like this: I script my opening sentence, the hardest one. It's going to start with, "Good evening, for those I have not met previously, my name is Jane McNeice and this evening I am going to tell you a little bit about my lived experience and how I came to do the work that I do today in mental health." That might come naturally to someone else, but for me it doesn't, so I script it, just like an actor would. When the audience hear it, it will seem like it is spontaneous. I need to know today what I am going to say on the 12th of September. The same goes for the next thirty-nine minutes and fifty-five seconds worth of dialogue. Yes, it will slightly shift each time I script, but the scripts tend to get better each time I rehearse them. I have read about Autistic actors who memorise scripts, then 'play' with the script. I play with the script too, in order to achieve my perfect version of it. The talk will go on to question and involve the audience and allow me to build a picture of who they are to work with them further. I can then be more creative and tailored. To prepare, I rehearse and recite the script over and over. I am currently at 30+ times, and it is the 12th of August, so by the time I deliver in September, it will have been scripted upwards of sixty times. The investment is worth it as I can pull the best elements together for other talks. I have another talk in October that I can morph this script into.

So, when do I rehearse my scripts? When alone. While out running, usually. I can measure the time it takes me to run so many miles, and match that with the script. I know where I need to be on my run when I finish my talk in my head.

> Note: the anchoring technique is also being used here, running outdoors has lots of visuals, and because I run the same route all the time, I can anchor the visual surroundings to points in my

story. Part of my story includes the time where I thought I had a personality disorder and sought out a psychiatrist to assess me. I know precisely where I should be on my running route at this point in my story, which is the roundabout near my local supermarket. I am in my head and subliminally anchoring to my visual surroundings. I am in a state of conscious unconsciousness, runners' flow, the alpha state. Effectively, I am shifting the dialogue away from my poor working memory to my long-term memory each time I rehearse the script, which works excellently. It's a good feeling doing it too.

Most people are aware that many Autistics struggle with 'small talk', and again, it's not that we cannot do small talk, it's just that we must put more effort into it. I have an Autistic script for small talk. I have learned that weather is okay to talk about, especially in the UK, but even in the UK, with British people, it is still possible to overdo it, so there is a line where the conversation must move on. Finding the line is sometimes difficult for me. I can usually tell in someone's eyes when I have overstepped it, and I promptly move on. One thing I will attempt to do is get past the small talk quickly or reduce the timeframe where small talk occurs to a window that allows for weather talk and little else. An example of this is prior to the start of a training course. I recognise that the social standard is to do small talk, so I can, and I do, but I want to get into the content and course as quickly as possible to get past the difficult part. Small talk is a fast depletion of control stocks and my energy. This overthinking of something that most others find easy is one of my biggest people challenges. When I don't know the person very well, or haven't met them before, I have no historical small talk to go on, so instead ask about things I can automatically know like their journey to the venue, did they find us okay, did they have a good evening, do anything nice – in most cases it will be an accurate presumption that they have travelled to the training, and guaranteed that they experienced an evening prior to that morning, etc. My focus is on them and themselves, which is easier for me during small talk. Otherwise, I shift to me and run the risk of talking too much, which I will be trying to avoid. The risk with small talk is running out of script, and there is only so much you can create with limited information, and my natural desire is to talk about my obsessions, so I will be holding back. What happens over time is the brain starts to become more resourceful and adept at finding things to talk about. If I am highly anxious, however, that will fail. If I'm in a place where the anxiety is under control, then my brain will fulfil the request.

Scripting allows me to be prepared, make more predictable something that would otherwise not be, to feel safe, to show interest in other people, and to aim to keep the conversation balanced, and not for me to immediately indulge in talk about my obsessions, which I can so easily do because they are fundamental to my life at all times. I do the same when meeting friends. I prepare for the conversations we might have, prepare for their response, which I often predict accurately due to my pattern spotting and predictions from the person's past responses, their values, attitudes, beliefs and our previous interactions. It simply allows order to the chaos I would otherwise be experiencing.

The result of all the scripting and all this effort is it looks impressive and natural to others, so I will be viewed as a confident and effective speaker. Again, another example of achieving high that will keep an unidentified autistic hidden.

I didn't have such coping mechanisms for a very long time, they have developed since addressing the gastric problems, when I was finally able to stop focusing on my digestive system for a moment.

For years, I wanted to speak but couldn't. I was silent in meetings, and absolutely dreaded any occasion where I would be asked to speak in front of a group. If forced, I would say something stupid and make myself look a fool or overthink the question or take it too literally. When I first went to work in the voluntary and community sector, I learned very quickly I would be required to attend a monthly team meeting, and a requirement of that meeting was for each attendee to update what they had been doing during the month. Standard team meeting stuff, but new to me. I had not experienced this before. The meetings made me ill. At the time, I was the personal assistant to the CEO, and as far as I was concerned, my job was to 'look after the CEO'. I saw this as a perfect summary of

STRENGTH *not* DEFECIT

what I did and had been doing, no inuendo intended, I just clearly knew my role, which was to support Martin as the CEO, so that he could support the wider team and the local third sector. I didn't work for a new and exciting project helping vulnerable people with innovative activities. That's precisely want I *wanted* to do! But of course, when you do the 'round robin (of creeping death)' in a meeting and it gets to you and you say, "I've been looking after Martin," you are going to get cackles, laughter and amusement from others, and the legacy laughter, which will reappear at every meeting thereafter. I hated those meetings with a vengeance.

Knowing I needed to verbally share my story effectively as well as through the written word, I sought the help of those who 'could'. I am rarely scared of seeking help from those who are amazing at what they do. Richard McCann is one of these people, an amazing public speaker, and someone who empowers others to do the same. For those of you making the connection to Wilma McCann, yes Richard McCann has his own tragic story, and a million other stories in between. He draws from his life story as to what is appropriate for the audience, and he is great at having you believe by the end of it that you 'CAN' too. Once wasn't enough for me with Richard, so this year I attended a second of his boot camps to brush up my speaking skills further. Richard has taught me some key skills for speaking my story, and while they mostly suit neurotypical ideals, e.g., good eye contact with the audience, I am willing to embrace many of them, even if they are not my ideal. What

Richard has been effective in doing is he has helped me to believe 'I can', which isn't easy. He forces me out of my speaker comfort zone and to present as confident, as if I really *am*. I love the illusion and I am more than happy to be fooled if it means I can achieve my own dream of success – finding lost people.

When I attended Richard's first Influence storytelling retreat, I cried watching a film Richard played. This is unlike me in a group setting, the social anxiety and fear of embarrassment prevents it on most occasions, my masks are solid, but with hindsight I recognise why – I had only been diagnosed seven weeks earlier, I was pre-menstrual (sorry for oversharing, but it played a part) and I watched a film about a boy who became a speaker and who had been non-verbal. He could have been me; he was me, and we connected. That was enough for it to happen – tears, a bit of time out, then okay and back in the room – physically and mentally. Today I recognise I had no voice for a very long time, even when people wanted me to have one. I just did not know 'why'. Medication for my gastric problems and then a slow building of confidence in public speaking changed that, but it is very much still a work in progress, and the confidence is fragile. What makes it possible (beyond the medication, and knowledge of the subject matter) is Autistic scripting and a good long-term memory that will hold the scripts, then dump them quickly when done with.

CHAPTER 12

Gaining a Corporate Edge through ~~Fortune-telling~~ Pattern Seeking

It is well documented that Autistics can often pick up on patterns, and quite quickly. This is one of the skills I had witnessed in myself for a very long time prior to diagnosis. The problem was I just couldn't fathom what it was I was doing.

For a long time, it felt like I was fortune-telling. I'd predict something was going to happen, and so forth it would come about. My predicting of death has my husband calling me the 'Grim Reaper'. It's not fortune-telling, nor is it supernatural, but today I see it as a combination of a couple of things: my higher levels of empathy and the feelings this generates, and my Autistic ability to pattern spot.

I pick up on patterns and pick up on them earlier than others might. A couple of examples I cannot necessarily explain are, firstly, a prediction of infertility in an ex-partner, which I ignored, and which was one of the more significant contributing factors to the demise of our relationship eleven years later. I have learned not to ignore my intuition and 'gut feeling' nowadays. I might question any substance it has at the time, and whether I am overreacting, but I now recognise I do have an ability to be correct more often than not, so I no longer ignore it, even if the trail of the pattern isn't clear. I guess my subconscious has it mapped out more deeply. The second example, in early February 2020, I'd picked up on a small amount of information about Covid-19 and worked out the pattern of what was to come. I'd crunched some numbers and made some notes in my phone, working out that by June 2020 we would have a major problem on our hands. I tried to warn others, which was received as overreacting, and promptly dismissed. I'd worked out the catastrophic impact it would have on one of my obsessions, my business, plus the health consequences and deaths that would occur. I still have the numbers I'd calculated in my phone. Of course, it is possible that my heightened anxiety alerts me to anything threatening, and as a broken clock is correct twice a day, I am going to be correct with some of the threats I predict, at some point, but it just feels more than that. It's correct more often than that.

More recently, I picked up on a downturn in training demand, mentioned it to peers in the industry, but no one else was seeing it. Eight weeks later, they were telling me, and by doing so confirmed that I had simply spotted it earlier than others.

This type of early prediction gives an excellent corporate advantage; it means I can adapt the business earlier to reflect any change(s). The business downturn could, in

STRENGTH *not* DEFECIT

fact, have been predicted by anyone. Training does not operate in a vacuum, and if the economy shrinks, so too will training demand, it's not rocket science. But what I was able to do, by spotting this early, was to work out which part of my business would shrink, and which areas would become more viable. I pushed the viable products, which for me were open courses rather than the more expensive closed in-house courses. While demand for closed courses reduced, businesses still recognised a need and commitment to mental well-being, and in a cost-of-living crisis, which often has an impact on employees' mental health, a greater demand for mental health training could even be expected. What they did is they booked what would be affordable, and perhaps what wouldn't have to be approved further up the corporate hierarchy. I filled my open courses during those months and largely compensated for lower demand in closed in-house courses. A full open course, while more labour intensive from an administration point of view, is financially more profitable than a closed course. But most importantly, every person trained is someone who can go on and support others in need who are likely suffering. Had I not picked up on the trend soon enough, the open courses would have clashed with the summer and would not have had the take-up they did.

My pattern spotting has a niche, its niche is people. It operates at both micro and macro level. I can spot patterns in the behaviour of individual people, making predictions about their behaviour based on patterns I have observed previously, and it also operates at a population-based level, with groups of people, but only where I have been exposed to the people or its population sufficiently. For example, it would fall short with a culture I understand less well or have been exposed to less often. I would need to know the cultural patterns to make a reliable prediction. In this case, it might only operate at a human level without being able to get below that.

For many years, my dream career was to become a psychological profiler. The plan after completing my degree in criminology was to join the police force, then undertake a master's degree in criminal or forensic psychology. I still believe my ability to pattern spot would have been well placed in crime detection and/or prevention. It's always interesting when I reflect on the myriad paths my life could have taken, but didn't, and not all of them were positive. For whatever reason, these paths were not meant for me.

My ability to visualise patterns is, I believe, a compensation for my lack of 'theory of mind'. Theory of mind is the human capacity and ability to predict what others are thinking, their desires, ignorance, empathy, perspective taking, emotions and intentions. It is believed that Autistics lack this theory of mind, to a greater or lesser degree. Essentially, we are referring to the ability to get into the mindset of someone else, and in many cases, to put our own frame of reference aside and to avoid judgement, particularly where empathy is concerned. In my own experience, I can do these things, but I am slower to process them than a neurotypical might be. For me, this historically has resulted in me being vulnerable to those with nefarious intentions, particularly because I also over-trust and overshare. I spot their ill intent and ulterior motives a little too late, like shutting the stable door after the horse has bolted, shall we say. I also don't think the ill-intention is always there at the beginning. I think it develops when people find my vulnerabilities and something about me they are not comfortable with. Sometimes it's the success, which in some people can cause jealousy. In my case, I believe my pattern spotting has been *acquired*, and it has been acquired to compensate for this deficit.

My human behaviour pattern spotting allows me to predict and act accordingly to give me a head start for the lack of theory of mind that I experience. Research suggests that those with average or higher intelligence can compensate for such challenges, in the same way that they might develop compensations for other challenges, such as social skills,[39] and I think this is what my brain has learned to do. Where the pattern seeking can contribute positively to one of my obsessions, additional motivation is there, and again we see the benefit of obsession in the driving seat.

As a pattern spotting Autistic, with a brain that does not switch 'off' about Autism, and has a burning need for answers, I can often work out a pattern where one exists. I overthink, process, ruminate and work out the connection, resulting in a theory or finding. The biggest challenge I have with this at the moment is that I am formulating theories before the science catches up to prove or deny them, or I work something out, then a research paper is published weeks later confirming my finding. I have three, possibly more, big theories at the moment that I don't believe the science has yet proven, but which my brain has. It could, of course, be that the science is out there, and I do not know about it. Without the science, asking others to take the leap of faith to believe you is very challenging, and it's incredibility difficult making a case for change with, "Well, you see, I was out running, when I had an aha moment, and this is what I've worked out … So, what we need to do is…" Yes, you can imagine the reaction. So, my only solution is to go back to university and prove my theories. One of my theories is a big one, it will not stack up without research, and even then, others might not listen. It will need others more influential, too.

I took the big decision this week, mid-August 2023, to apply to go back to university to test my theories out. My burning desire is to prove the theories I believe to be true; the qualifications will be a by-product of the research I want to perform. Yet, I don't know if I will be given a place, and it won't be easy studying alongside my other obsession, my business, but I figure that I think about Autism all the time anyway, so I may as well do it in a more structured way that achieves something better for the Autistic community. My belief in something bigger than me also has me thinking, *Don't worry, the universe will find a way*. Hopefully that won't turn out to be naïve thinking on my part.

CHAPTER 13

Anxiety: Harnessing the Power of Discomfort

From an early age, my nemesis was anxiety. It hasn't left my side since the age of three. As my earliest memories started, so too did the anxiety. This coincided with my departure from the protection of my parents, mostly my mum's care, and exposure to people, strangers and close proximity environment. My commencement in nursery was when the anxiety started, and it has never gone away, not entirely. I have slivers of time when it does, one is when I read, and the other is when I have been away, usually overseas, on holiday, and for the first day when I come home it's gone, I cannot connect with it, it's gone. The following day, like an old friend, it returns, after a very short-lived respite. I've considered what it is about the change which causes the cessation, whether it is the comfort of being back in the familiar, I just do not know. Outside of this, it never goes away.

Everyone knows what anxiety feels like, anything that puts you out of your comfort zone can cause feelings of anxiety – purposeful performance anxiety, for example, a job interview, test, screening of some kind, there are plenty of examples. This we regard as *normal* anxiety. When the fear 1) has **longevity** – disproportionate to the threat or still there when the threat has gone away, 2) is **severe**, and 3) is having an **impact** on day-to-day living, then it's not normal anxiety. At this point, it's very likely an anxiety disorder. However, it could also be a comorbid or co-existing anxiety, that which is attached to another factor, such as Autism or other neurodivergence. Not all Autistics experience this comorbid, but many Autistics do. To give you an idea of what my anxiety feels like, it's like constantly feeling you are about to fall downstairs. It never goes away, but it's been there for so long I don't know a life without it. It is my normal.

My anxiety peaks in highly demanding social situations, and just like anyone else, when I step out of my comfort zone. My comfort zone is large. Why? Simply because I stretch it. I keep going and doing the things that scare me the most. Because I do them daily, it becomes less scary, and so they move into my comfort zone. One thing I am aware of, however, is that the fear of something can return if I don't continue to face it, so the only way to keep it at bay is to keep doing the things that scare me. If I have a temporary cessation in public speaking or training, for example, my anxiety about it returns and increases. If I was to stop doing this and go after comfort and safety, I would become a recluse, and I totally understand Autistics who choose that life for themselves. I also recognise it may not have been chosen *by* them, but rather *for* them, through marginalisation and ostracising. After the summer training break – training demand is quiet during summer – the first few courses in September will cause me higher than usual levels of anxiety. I regain my sensitivity to it.

I don't commend myself on many things in life, but one thing I do commend myself on is bravery, to step out of my comfort zone time and time again, daily. I observe people who sit back in their comfortable space and stay there, never daring to try something that causes any level of discomfort unless an external force causes this. That's totally fine, it's a safe place to be, but what I loathe is when those same people arrogantly claim how resilient and fantastic they are at managing stress, when in fact it's more the case that it's untested. I see this in a pronounced way with parents of neurotypical children who subtly (and sometimes directly) infer their parenting skills are superior to other parents. I often think, raise a child with additional needs for sixteen years, then tell me you feel the same way. Yes, they might still feel fantastic, but they also might not, the truth is they won't ever know because it either didn't happen to them (chance), or they didn't seek the challenge, e.g., fostering or adopting a child with special needs. The results are all relative. The only thing I hope you can take from my story is that if you are willing, with effort and bravery, you *can* do it.

Sometimes, of course, we are forced out of our comfort zone, it's not a choice. I am forced out of my comfort zone every single day when I interact with humanity. I don't live off grid, and I am not self-sufficient, so my basic needs won't be met if I do not interact or co-operate. It's incredibly uncomfortable for me as an Autistic person – the call to the GP, going to the shops and speaking to the assistant at the checkout, just being around people in a proximity environment. I am overly familiar with permanent discomfort, maybe even desensitised because of this. The discomfort doesn't ever go away, people haven't suddenly become part of my comfort zone, I have simply got used to the discomfort of being out of it. That said, I am yet to master the discomfort associated with conflict – that's another level for me and very much work in progress. I think that will come in time, as my self-esteem and self-worth continue to improve. I'm only two years post-diagnosis, so it's like starting anew, like you might support a toddler to learn to value themselves.

When I am exposed to anxiety-provoking situations, particularly conflict, I often adopt the flight (or flee) response. That does not mean I literally flee, or run, as in most situations I cannot, but it can take the form of avoidance. When I cannot avoid, I fawn.

Fawn is to please and appease, as seen in my people pleasing behaviour. I can't avoid you, so I will deal with the threat of you by pleasing and not ruffling your feathers, so to speak, sometimes the charm offensive. I overly apologise, fail to exert necessary boundaries, and I take on the responsibility for *your* feelings. Now, I *have* to say, I am very much in the process of change. That starts with acknowledging my trauma and threat response. From here on in, I am working to counter it – without apology. He (she, or they) who attempts to capitalise on knowing my weak spot could find a very different response to what they expect.

I have fears, lots of fears, fear of the known and fear of the unknown, and day-after-day, I step into that abyss anyway, because I will not let it win. The moment I stop doing that, it wins, and my comfort zone will shrink. And it would shrink small. The safest space for me is home, away from the world, where I could all too easily hide away forever. The allure is comforting. But what would that achieve? An existence, at best. Limiting my engagement with the world to absolute necessity and basic need is a life not well spent. I have far too many things I want to achieve in life, things that require me to interact for the benefit of myself and for others, my husband, my children, my clients, people who are suffering and in need. A life without purpose is for me not a life, and I would not want to be here, so as long as I have dreams, a purpose and a family, I need to be brave.

I've learned a lot from being brave. I've learned that exposure helps. For example, the more I deliver training or publicly speak, the easier it becomes. Psychologists call this the 'mere exposure effect',[40] which does as its title suggests. I've learned the skills and coping mechanisms needed to achieve in my life and in my work, how to make a difference, and I feel they would be wasted if not put to good use. I fought and worked incredibly hard for them, especially as an undiagnosed Autistic for half of my life, so that effort would also have been a waste. My bravery comes from my determination, and with determination, we can overcome deficits that we might otherwise not, and that otherwise would disable us.

CHAPTER 14

Self-care for All Business Owners, Especially for Autistic Ones!

Like many Autistics, I am prone to burnout, and while this doesn't happen often, I always need to be mindful that it is one of my greatest threats, primarily because I am Autistic, and secondly because I am an Autistic that likes to do *a lot!*

Like with many life experiences, Autistics experience burnout in an amplified way, often specifically referred to as 'Autistic burnout'. While unique to each Autistic, the National Autistic Society defines Autistic burnout as:

> *… a syndrome conceptualised as resulting from chronic life stress and a mismatch of expectations and abilities without adequate supports. It is characterised by pervasive, long-term (typically 3+ months) exhaustion, loss of function, and reduced tolerance to stimulus.*
>
> National Autistic Society [online][41]

Autistic people describe lots of characteristics of burnout, including impact on their mental and physical health, and how others respond to them burning out, which sadly often includes a lack of empathy from neurotypicals (the double empathy problem[42]). For me, Autistic burnout looks like depression – loss of enjoyment in the things I usually enjoy, pronounced fatigue and energy loss, and a pervasive low mood, which for me includes suicidal ideation. The latter alone makes it worth preventing. For a long time, I simply thought I was having bouts of depression alongside my anxiety, but my symptoms don't last long enough to be an episode of depression, which on average would be six to eight months. The symptoms for me last about three to four weeks. They are acute and chronic in nature, but not in longevity. Shorter longevity could well be why I have managed through life without the burnouts having too much of an impact. They're not long enough to dramatically affect my working life, or relationships, etc., but they would be if they were more frequent. Because of the high stress vulnerability, which is the case for many Autistics, to prevent frequency, I must manage my 'Stress Bucket'.[43]

All human beings are trying to prevent their stress buckets from overflowing, to avoid both physical and mental illness. For me, it's avoiding the Autistic burnout that contributes to both. It's very possible that I have a smaller stress bucket than most, or that there is too much going in there and too quickly, or perhaps a combination of these. I actually believe it's the pace at which stress is going in there. The things I find stressful as an Autistic will also be different to the things a neurotypical might find stressful. Like anyone else, provided my self-care is prioritised and matches the level at which stress is going into my bucket, then my bucket won't overflow. Because lots of stress goes in there, I need a really effective release valve that flows efficiently, and fast.

If it does overflow, there is only one real solution to recovery from burnout, which is quite simply… REST! Of course, we could add other considerations pertinent to Autistics (and in fact to everyone), like adequate support systems, routine, etc., but the only part largely in our control is getting some rest time, and that is not always in your control when you have small children you are responsible for, who still require *their* needs to be met, whether you are burned-out or not. When I do get the chance to rest, I recover, quickly, and I have the energy to get back on the carousel of life and carry on. This, of course, is a very reactive way of managing burnout. What we all really need is to be proactive.

Proactively managing burnout – that is, preventing it in the first place – is the best solution of all and something that I attempt to do daily. However, one of the mistakes I had made for a very long time was to talk the talk, but not walk the walk. I always liked the idea of better 'balance' and talked about it being my single biggest challenge between work and home life but failed to properly put plans behind the idea to achieve it. When an obsession becomes successful, it can become overwhelming, and *even* when it is our obsession, if it becomes overwhelming, it stops being pleasurable, and that's when it can fizzle out, or burn us out, the place I was at just before Covid-19 hit.

My desire for balance had no authentic intention pre-diagnosis. Recognition of this came on the back of reading a lived experience story about someone with an eating disorder, who said they too had become successful in what they do, needed to slow down, did not want to be solely remembered for their work in mental health rather than for them as a person, so they worked on several things they needed to do in order to change that. They put a plan together. Reading their story taught me I had no plan, that's what I was missing, and why I wasn't achieving the balance I wanted. So, that's what I proceeded to do, at the start of 2023, I developed a plan. It was a New Year's Resolution that I continue to administer today. I put several actions in place, and all of these are forms of self-care that amount to my goal of achieving a healthy balance between work and home:

- Absolutely NOTHING gets booked in on my day off unless it is a total investment in self. This is a decompression day (with the exception of parenting responsibilities).
- No more than three course deliveries, or sessions of delivery, by me in a week.
- Give myself time before replying to emails and requests (especially where an important decision is required).
- Use management practices that create ease of management, not that just keep others happy.
- Stop oversharing, be more reticent, not everyone is your friend. Protect yourself.

- Don't plan back-to-back training deliveries – make time for emails between courses and sessions.
- Go to bed early and try to get five five-mile runs in each week, first thing when it's not too 'peopley' outdoors.
- If it is a running 'rest day', try to do fifteen minutes of meditation instead (subject to interruptions from children) – the brain needs time in alpha every day, not just the running days, especially when I demand so much of it in beta!
- Don't book more than one meet-up with a friend in a four-week period.
- Try to ensure weekends are only spent with immediate family – those with whom I do not need to mask – my husband, two boys and my daughter. Weekends are protected decompression time.
- Ensure the downtime of Christmas, Easter and summer holidays *is* downtime rather than work or over-planning festivities with too many people; sub-contract any training bookings during this time to Mind Matters associates unless the courses are ones where only I am qualified to deliver them.
- Quit feeling guilty for doing all that, quit trying to be all things to all people and people pleasing – it's okay to say "no" to others and instead say "yes" to me. I *am* worth it!

These are my commandments. I am trying to stick to them, and though it isn't always easy (or achieved), having them written down helps as a mental reminder to the commitment I made to myself. It makes it more likely that 'balance' *will* be achieved. Just reading them again now reminds me how important they are if I am to prevent burnout.

Whether Autistic or not, we all need to ensure we don't burnout. The World Health Organization recognised burnout as a significant health issue when it expanded the definition in the ICD-11 (international classification of diseases), and while it does not specifically class it as a medical condition, it describes it as a workplace phenomenon where continued workplace stress has not been addressed.[44] The contributories in *Autistic* burnout are usually much wider than the workplace, referenced as 'chronic life stress' in the NAS definition,[45] but for many of us the burnout will still be linked to work, even if that work exists because it morphed out of an obsession that we love. This again is where an unidentified or undiagnosed autistic may experience burnout but not yet have learned they were always more prone to it because they were (are) Autistic. They may even be downplaying their burnout, comparing it to the type of burnout everyone else experiences, rather than Autistic burnout, a bit like comparing an everyday low mood to depression. Knowing you are more prone is a good reminder that extra protection is required. It reminds us to be vigilant and proactive, and to prioritise our self-care.

Self-care is a very individual thing. I've shared with you *my* goal, and *my* roadmap to get me there, but for others it may look very different. My challenge is I don't have an 'off' button in my head. If I try to switch off, the thoughts of 'doing' just pop back in, so I need a strict plan, and even then, it may not be successful.

Setting up and running a small business can feel like a lonely place, as can delivering mental health training and being away from home some nights in what are often sterile, characterless hotel rooms. I have my coping mechanisms for managing how I feel about that. One that I make regular use of is the solitude this affords, so I always do a fifteen-minute meditation in a morning when I am away from home and have no children or canine interruptions, and I have an early night and read. For a long time, I did things very lone-wolf, apart from a few digital communications, and during the 2020 lockdowns I made three valuable decisions: 1) seek further therapy, 2) get assessed for Autism, and 3) find a business coach with whom I am comfortable working.

My business coach is Sarah Brown of Inspire2Aspire (www.inspire2aspire.co.uk). I'd sampled the thirty-minute talks with other coaches and franchises, but felt they were very much the 'stick' of the 'carrot and stick'. Some business owners will relish this, someone holding them to account, making sure they 'do'. I don't need this, I am more self-motivated than they likely are, but what I did need, and what was well overdue, was someone to talk through ideas, issues, plans, systems and a good listener – Sarah Brown does all of that and more. She comes from the 'leave the world a better place than you found it' school of thinking that I share, and of course while I acknowledge it can be useful to have a coach who thinks differently to you, I value the fact that Sarah is ethical, cares, wants to achieve equity, and quite simply knows her stuff. She's smart! Sarah is one of my best business decisions to date. My others were my associate pool, and having my daughter come to work for me.

Laura dramatically reduces the risk of my burnout, as well as having to ensure she too doesn't burnout. Laura's family have a huge amount going on, four children with additional needs, a husband and father who works long days and is sometimes away overnight, and Laura juggles lots of balls – medical and school appointments, work, and trying to maintain a semblance of health herself. Her challenges can be quite disabling, and yet she is able to continue to work. Why? Because we are one another's supports. Both of our families are complex, and because of this, we are rarely able to offer the practical support to each other that is needed, but what we are pretty good at is 'checking-in' and allowing the other to offload while the other listens. Every single day I am reminded that what most people need is simply to be listened to, with understanding, without judgement, and with a good measure of empathy. She can't fix my challenges, nor can I hers, but neither of us is asking for that, nor do we expect it. We just need a good listener.

In the last year, I have felt the benefit of building and investing in relationships. I have always kept prompt regular contact with my clients, and delivered on our promises, but one thing I have not actively engaged in is face-to-face networking. All my networking up to the last year has been digital, through the written word because, as I've already highlighted, this is my path of least resistance, and where I am most comfortable. But a few months ago, I attended a women in business networking event as a speaker, and in doing so was invited to another local women's group – welcome into my world the Sherwood Ladies! Yes, as in Robin Hood, as we meet at a venue near Sherwood Forest in Nottinghamshire, historical home of the outlaw and his merry men.

Sherwood Ladies is a relatively small group, so not too overwhelming for me. There is a nominated speaker from the group at each meeting, opportunities to talk and network, and a lovely meal afterwards. It's relaxed, friendly and the first networking group I have felt nearly comfortable with. I didn't want a weekly meeting; I don't have the time for weekly. I didn't want a breakfast meeting. I don't eat breakfast, and I prefer to be out running having created alone time and being in my head, but I do want to interact with humanity, sometimes. Of course, I connect with my learners every single time I deliver training, that's a given, but this is something different for me. When I deliver training, my purpose is clear, when I socialise, it is not. This networking group feels much more on my terms, and fits with my busy world. The ladies have given me a great opportunity to share my lived experience at the next meeting in September, so I am looking forward to connecting with them a little more. I feel quite proud of myself when I do something like this, because this is the sort of thing that really does test me and my comfort zone.

A lot of people don't like forced 'networking', so imagine how that feels when you are Autistic! It is exhausting.

Self-care starts at a very basic level, having basic needs met, and as I highlighted with Maslow's [Autistic] hierarchy of needs, my obsessions are a fundamental part of this. This being the case, my greatest form of self-care is to have the time and space to indulge my obsessions. This, of course, I try to balance too. My husband and children have needs, so making sure my husband has time for the things he's passionate about and enjoys – cars, mountain biking and gaming – or time out with his friends, and making sure our children's needs are met is also important to me. Sadly, I live with a great deal of guilt that I fall short on a lot of these, but I try to remind myself that I have historically internalised neurotypical ideals of marriage and motherhood, not Autistic ones, and mine are different. I am 'normal' for an Autistic wife and mother and can only be judged and held to this standard. I cannot un-Autistic myself, much as society might like me to. My family are loved, I work hard not to neglect, desperately try to balance it all, and try hard not to feel guilty for falling short.

Self-care for me will rarely be a spa day – now and again, maybe. My daughter and I have both agreed that if we were to wait for this kind of self-care, we would be very disappointed. We can't do the mother and daughter stuff many mums and daughters do together because we don't have the levels of childcare support that permit this, but one day we may get our spa date together. But we recognise we are lucky, we get 'moments' – moments where we drink a cup of tea while it's still hot, moments to sit in the garden for ten minutes with a little peace and silence, solo drives to the supermarket where we are alone for thirty minutes and decompress, precious moments that add up to reducing the 'chronic life stress' that otherwise threatens our Autistic existence.

Maybe, like me, you too are an employer, and you manage people who are Autistic and want to support them more effectively, so they don't experience Autistic burnout, or maybe you recognise the things that benefit Autistic employees will benefit *all* employees and prevent others from burning out. There's a lot you can do to support them and their self-care:

- **Always ask, never assume** about strengths or deficit in Autistics or anyone else for that matter. Ask about needs.
- Invite us to social events and keep inviting us, even if we continually decline. One day we may say yes and feel able to, and even if that never happens, **we still want to *feel* included**.
- Ensure each employee has some form of **personal well-being support plan** tailored to their specific well-being needs. This is especially important for Autistics, but also for other employees too.
- **Offer flexible working.** Do all tasks need to be undertaken between nine and five, or in the workplace? Could they be done from home or during the night

(Autistics and those with ADHD are often nocturnal and work productively at night)?
- **Become an ally**: Listen (and hear) Autistic stories, educate yourself, speak out and advocate for your Autistic colleagues. Become an Autism or neurodiversity champion via the organisations which offer this. As I hope to have illustrated, you will more than likely employ more neurodivergent people than you currently realise.
- If you want a way in, to connect with your Autistic employees, the door is titled **'obsessions (SPINS)'**. Indulge them, support them and please don't put us in a position where we feel we have to mask them.
- And of course, **find our strengths, don't let 'ableism' be your blind spot** preventing you from seeing these. With support, Autistics, just like anyone else, can overcome many challenges, and when you have forgotten about the support, we will still remember it. What you will get back in return is loyalty, commitment and the effort that goes with that. To this day, I can remember every single occasion of support and every person who has supported me, the helpful comment, or act of kindness. I would return it a million times over. Most times they didn't do it because I was Autistic – I've only known I am for two years – they did it because it was the *right* thing to do.

"But my darling, you being different… was your strength all along."

N.R. Hart

Epilogue

Many Autistics go unidentified and undiagnosed, and many of us do so *precisely* because we are successful by neurotypical standards. This success is achieved because of one key Autistic strength that overcomes the challenges of living in the neurotypical society that disables us – determination! The determination does not invalidate or remove the challenges, it is the driver that permits us to overcome them, and in many cases, to supersede what others will achieve, based on the ideals others created that we internalised, despite the fact we were, and are, and always have been, 'different'.

That determination caused us to be extremely resourceful, and to develop effective coping mechanisms for our challenges and disabilities, coping mechanisms that have allowed us to achieve success despite having a condition that others claim 'limits' us. To find the remaining undiagnosed autistics is to learn from them, learn what coping mechanisms they have used that work, and to be able to teach these to younger Autistics, or Autistics who are still struggling and need more ideas and solutions for their challenges. What works for one won't always work for others, but I don't just have one coping mechanism, I have hundreds, many in operation most of the time. There is a wide menu to choose from! These coping mechanisms aid my survival on a daily basis and could aid the survival of other Autistics too. My coping mechanisms won't just be effective for Autistic people, they could also be effective for neurotypicals, so again neurodiversity stands to benefit if we are all found.

Society continues to have a pervasive view of Autism, largely linked to disability and deficit, with marginal allowance for a spike of genius or islet of ability. So when society sees, reads, or hears about someone who appears all-round highly successful – Autistics who likely have several obsessions, whose obsessions are all of a socially acceptable nature, powerful enough to overcome their disabilities, and to achieve high success – Autism becomes a million light years from their thinking, including in the minds of the undiagnosed autistic themselves, who are also exposed to and influenced by these ableist views.

The more successful the unidentified autistic becomes, the more tolerance they might get for their authentic self – direct, unfiltered, questioning, for example – but there are no guarantees. It also then becomes less likely that those around them will question the presence of Autism, colleagues who may now be junior to them and not feel able to. In my career history, I came across a very high tolerance of negative behaviour from a paediatric consultant in a hospital whose success, and the hospital's need for their skills, permitted appalling conduct from them towards colleagues, which otherwise would not have been tolerated and would most definitely have constituted bullying. Had that person have worked in a coffee shop, I am pretty sure they would have been dismissed. I have no idea whether that consultant was Autistic, but what I am saying is tolerance sometimes changes where success is present, and that tolerance (and in this case fear of the person) could also prevent identification.

Ableism has an impact on the known disabled, but also those who would not otherwise be viewed as disabled. These are some of the views which misled and still mislead unidentified autistics into believing they are neurotypical (and their continuing to try to live as this) when they are not. Society assumes all human beings to be neurotypical, an unwritten birthright, until there is irrefutable proof otherwise. This assumption creates a blind spot until the person learns there are alternatives and the traits of these other neurotypes. It's bit like assuming everyone has blue eyes then learning that some are brown.

The ableist views of Autism infer and communicate 'incapable', so human beings mistakenly learn you must be incapable to be Autistic, and so those who appear hyper-capable become the societal blind spot. I was in that blind spot for forty-four years until my own self-identification, my misleadings being 'You finished school **successfully**', 'You run a **successful** business' and 'You've **successfully** raised a family', etc. The thinking is only challenged when the undiagnosed autistic burns-out or becomes unwell, i.e., they stop being capable of functioning at their usual levels, they stop presenting as *successful*. Only then do they or others start to question 'why'. This should not be the way we find Autistic people. Often, a range of other causes will be grasped at and clung to first – I was adopted, I was abused, I have anxiety, I have been exposed to trauma of some kind (Autistics often carry trauma anyway), it is because I am gay, or it is because I am a person of colour, and a range of other identity determinants and/or acute life events are seen as the answer to 'why'. For some, that will totally be the explanation for their suffering, but for others, it may be an over attribution, or in some cases a false attribution. They may cling so much to this preferred narrative that they create a blind spot to any other underlying factor(s), and for some, but not all, Autism (or perhaps ADHD, or both) will be their answer, or an additional answer, to 'why'.

Autism would likely explain their experiencing of these other things as more challenging than others might experience them. Understanding other underlying factors can help to understand these other experiences. In fact, if we take abuse as just one example, we know based on the research that there is a heightened risk factor of being a victim of abuse in Autistic people,[46] so it would be common for an Autistic to be attached to an abuse or victim narrative of some kind. Finding out we are Autistic can help us to process and understand why these things happened to us in the first place – that we were vulnerable – and why we have experienced them in such a profound way, maybe why they became a cause we fought tirelessly for, or ended up working in. I didn't find a career in mental health, it found me because of my life experience and my past. It was testimony to a woman searching for an answer in mental illness, and not wanting others to suffer like she had, just like my degree in criminology previous to that was testimony to me searching for my identity in the criminal fraternity because I thought I was bad and had something wrong with me. Put simply, no one is looking for us, not even ourselves, if we don't uncover this blind spot.

In my own case, I was searching desperately for my 'why', but I most definitely wasn't looking for the answer in neurodivergence. My own ableist views at the time and no knowledge of non-stereotypical Autism prevented that. I found it by chance. Only then did I take the time and interest to learn what I didn't know, and I am still doing that every single day. Our learning who we are should not be a lottery, or game of chance, it should be a fundamental human right. All the signs were there – a cycle of burnouts, pervasive anxiety that never goes away, living with managed suicidal thoughts and severe gastrointestinal problems, plus the chequered and 'unusual' life story, my 'outliers' – but the **success** hid it all to others, that's what they saw (the focus on the highs not the lows), and yet I was relying on these others to find me. Perhaps most importantly, what I could not see, but what I would later learn, was that the success existed BECAUSE I am Autistic. Today I am in no doubt whatsoever that my success exists because of this very fact. I have quite literally only come to that realisation in the last two months.

Like many, I trusted the 'professionals' to find me, I believed them capable, the people with the answers, the knowledge and the credentials to do so. They were the successful, the 'experts', not me. This was an oversight on my part, a blind spot too.

What is happening right now is a seismic shift, a wrong is being put right, a wrong that was and is both a health inequality and a women's issue. Lots of women – and men and non-binary, but mostly women, as they were the ones who were (and still are) most often missed – are finding out they are Autistic. Why? Because they are no longer reliant solely on 'professionals' to find them. They are working it out for themselves. Ableism is, and has been, causing us harm, just like all the other 'ism's which exist, the difference here being that we don't expose or talk about ableism as much as the other 'ism's. Stimulating a discourse about ableism is causing many to acknowledge its existence, and to challenge it. This is increasing. In part, this is due to the numbers, the number of voices shouting about the impact of ableism are growing because more and more people are learning they are Autistic. I anticipate that is only going to increase further in the next ten years. Reliance on the need for a professional to be the one to find us has been removed, until the point of Autism assessment (assuming the person wishes to be diagnosed and not just to self-identify). What has replaced the professional in the earlier stages is the power of the people. We are finding and identifying ourselves.

Social media has brought the information to the masses, via lived experience stories like my own, Autism organisations sharing key information about non-stereotypical Autism and other vast information sharing. The letters after names no longer matter until point of assessment. What matters is connecting the right information with those that need it, and this is currently happening *en masse*, via TikTok, LinkedIn, Facebook, Instagram and X (formerly known as Twitter). I appreciate not all the information is perfectly accurate, but not all of it needs to be if enough of it is and the output is high. The criticisms that can be thrown at social media also apply to *all* information sharing, including that derived from professionals, and some of those sharing and communicating on social media will in fact *be* qualified professionals. We just presume most of *their* communication to be accurate because we hold it in higher esteem than information from non-professionals. This was the fundamental mistake I made. Social media is simply another mode of communicating information, just like 'word of mouth', TV, radio, magazines, journal articles, clinical appointments, or otherwise. And my business illustrates that when enough mud is thrown at a wall, some of it will definitely stick. The more we know about the make-up of mud and the texture of the wall, the more we understand it, the more likely it is to do that!

With all its criticisms – which are often the reverse of the same coin – social media has been very successful in reaching lots of people, globally, and quickly, and allows 'the man on the Clapham omnibus' to put his/her/their information out *themselves*. It is largely under *their* control. Unlike what we see on TV, radio, or in the press, where the owners and industry regulators hold a lot of the power and choose the speakers, social media provides another dimension – the power is in the user's hands. We decide the topic, we decide when, we decide how, and we have the tools to make it 'reach' based on what we know and learn through being a user, or learning from other users whose knowledge is more advanced than ours (in my case, my daughter who will very often give me little hints and tips). The only part we do not control is how it is received and interpreted, and any rules we must follow put in place by the platform owners, who are largely unregulated. It is because of this freedom that it also has the power to do harm, but that is no different to me doing harm by walking up to someone in the street and communicating a harmful comment or showing them triggering images. The medium is not intrinsically good or bad, it is the content communicated and how we communicate it that makes it so.

The current result of wide social media coverage of non-stereotypical Autism is a surge in non-stereotypical undiagnosed autistic people self-identifying and going to their GP seeking assessment because they now have their missing number 3) non-stereotypical Autism information, which completes the criteria for self-identification. The information reached them, in all senses of the word. Some will end up being assessed through the NHS if in the UK, or through private assessment, and that will of course lead to an increase in the numbers of people who are known Autistic and therefore an increase in the Autistic voice. I'll add to that by saying we will likely be passionate

EPILOGUE

about having a voice (in whatever way they communicate) because the late diagnosed are going to be making up for a significant amount of lost time, and our voices will in many cases be driven by the pain, suffering and grief of being lost for that time.

If you haven't already heard it, the response you will hear from society will be along the lines of, "There was none of this Autism in my day," or, "Everyone wants a label nowadays," or, "We were all *all 'right'* in our day," or, "Everyone needs to be in a box," and the classic, "We are *all* on the Autistic spectrum anyway." I'm not even going to go there with the last one as I promised you not to repeat my last book! Social media will, of course, be one of the 'things' blamed and scapegoated for this increased number.

> Note: the person was always Autistic, they were just hidden. Above all else, I really want you to remember this key point: How many Autistics self-identify, through social media or otherwise, is illustrative of the level of damage that has been done, not how many people want a label. The number in this group will be the very people who could have been but were failed to be found by professionals – health, social care and education – the late diagnosed. Late identified/diagnosed Autistics are a measure of society's failure to find and support us every time it had the chance. If a million people are added to the Autistic number, then that's a million people (late diagnosed) who got missed, went without support

and suffered for it. A million failures, a million damages.

Blame isn't helpful, but change is, so rather than focus on blaming, we need to focus on change and preventing this missing of Autistic people in the future, particularly girls and women. Social media is not the enemy here, it has just removed the need for a 'professional' to be the only person who can find us in the first instance. What you are seeing is *empowerment*, the people have been empowered through information sharing to work it out for themselves, and the kickback you will see, which in some cases will be from those very professionals, might be them trying to protect their *own* qualifications, livelihood and success.

Of course, not all self-identifications will be correct, and (based on the current socially constructed pathologising system for diagnosis) only a formal assessment by a suitably qualified professional can prove one way or another, but many will not be wrong. We are an intelligent group of people, and our intelligence will be one of the very variables that will make it more likely we *are* correct when we do work it out for ourselves.

My diagnosis – which came about because I found myself via a social media post of fewer than ninety words in less than sixty seconds – means I am now more aware of the deficits I can and have overcome, the limits that I should not exceed when my psychological and/or physical safety is at risk, and how to protect myself from the threats associated with my Autistic profile. Most of all, I am aware

EPILOGUE

of my levels of determination, what my determination can achieve when it is linked to an Autistic obsession, and how all of my successes were successful because they were, or are, my Autistic obsessions.

I am determined to do several things in the coming years, and today, knowing the secret to success and the fact that I have been harbouring it in abundance through obsession, I can, for the very first time ever in my life, know with confidence that I *will* achieve them. Never before has that been the case for me. Something has changed within me. I have three theories I want to test out empirically, one which has the potential to change mental health services as we currently know them. Whether that happens will come down to several factors, including proving my theory(s) correct with reliable and valid research. But it will also come down to whether anyone is listening, and the willingness on the part of others to make changes based on the findings. Some of that is out of my control but I won't ever stop trying to influence it.

Autistics will sometimes work things out before the science catches up. I believe the science has not yet tested out the things I wish to, and only by me doing so empirically (and proving my theories correct) will I have a fighting chance of getting someone to listen. This is me making noise. Until I was found on the 22nd of June 2021, I made none. Imagine a million or more other Autistic voices desperate to be heard and fighting for change, maybe two or three million, not just a community, but a movement. Watch this space…

STRENGTH *not* DEFECIT

In the last fifteen years, I have watched mental illness go from the elephant in the room to being something that the world is talking about, something that is far more normalised. Today, I predict the same change that we have seen in mental health happening with Autism, ADHD and other neurodivergence. I give it ten to fifteen years, and I am so looking forward to watching it happen and being part of that change.

High achievement is the very reason so many women in my generation have been missed. No one pathologises high achievement, it is not seen as 'wrong' but rather 'right', so others are blind to what drives it, and no one is ever looking for the driver to be Autism. Based on what I have learned and pattern spotted in the last two years, my belief is the biggest group of hidden undiagnosed autistics is middle-aged and older women, who are exceptionally high achievers, at the top of their game, but at the same time will be feeling that they just 'don't fit' or something 'isn't quite right'. Remove ableism and we will find them. They are already high achievers in many cases, imagine what they could achieve with added awareness, acceptance and support. If this group of people continues to be missed, the whole of neurodiversity loses out. We lose out on their voice, their stories, their experiences of the world, their different ways of viewing the world. We might not maximise or capitalise on their ability to see patterns, and learn from their coping mechanisms, or problem solve in ways that are different to others. That's a big loss for us all.

I didn't high achieve because I am a highly athletic

or a highly intellectual person. I high achieved because my achievements have been, or still are, my Autistic obsessions and they are driven by Autistic perseverance and determination. Autistics high achieve in the things we obsess about. When desired outcomes are powered by Autistic level obsession, they naturally become achievements, the very achievements that will keep us hidden, so we instead become labelled 'high achievers' and presumed capable. The very place you should be looking for the non-stereotypical Autistic is in capability, high achievement and high success, and the very place you *are* looking for us is in deficit and incapability. You are not even warm.

When high achievement is met with ableism, Autistic people get missed, unless the high achiever breaks... We shouldn't have to break to be found. We are few now because most of us are still hidden, because everyone is looking in the wrong place, or looking in the right place, but not making the connection. I got lucky early on in this journey of change, but I'm going back to help the rest of my people because I know their pain. The hidden non-stereotypical Autistics may well offer neurodiversity another story and narrative different to what we currently know, and most of us have a lot of time to make up for!

Acknowledgements

Invariably I will miss someone who is utterly deserving of my thanks, as there are many who have, and continue to, support my endeavours to raise awareness of non-stereotypical Autism and the life experiences of the late diagnosed. Nevertheless, there are those who, without their presence in my world, I would not in any way be able to achieve what I do today.

My first thanks go to my husband Steven. Our world is not an easy one, but since our unison in 2009, we have ploughed through the challenges like an ice-breaker ship, aptly titling ourselves the *ice-boat truckers*. Where would I be without you?!

Secondly, thanks to my daughter Laura, who equally understands each and every challenge, and knows one hundred percent why I do this and why all of this is so important to me, never once questioning why I continue to fight for justice, even when I am totally exhausted by doing so.

Thank you to my two boys who teach me so much every single day, Ben showing me how to love and believe in yourself, and Oliver reminding me there are a million different ways to experience the world, and the Autistic way is merely different. My family (including my four amazing grandchildren – Evie, Bella, Violet and Sebastian) make living as an Autistic in a neurotypical world survivable.

Thank you to my parents, Susan and Brian, who only saw my strengths, and by doing so played a huge part in what I have achieved, and to my late brother Robert who showed me that it's not about whether others believe in you, it's about whether *you* believe in you.

Thank you to Jen my editor who has painstakingly read my manuscript and found detail I didn't even know existed – her eye for this is awe inspiring!

Thank you to my advance readers who have taken time out of their world to share my world, in particular Jackie Schuld, Hayley Graham, Dan Fell at Doncaster Chamber and Dr Luke Beardon at Sheffield Hallam University, who took the time between lectures and work to read my book (…and whose reading of it filled me with as much fear and trepidation as it did excitement!).

Thank you to my associate trainers at Mind Matters – Gemma, Tara, Adrian, Sarah, Ivy, Bill and others – who help us to do what we do better, and invariably support Mind Matters as a vehicle for positive change in mental health and, of late, in our endeavours to bring positive change to knowingly neurodivergent, and unknowingly neurodivergent, people. Thank you also to Sarah Brown, my business coach, who is an ally to so many, and most definitely to me.

Most of all, thank you to everyone who has taken the time (and expense) to indulge my book beyond the

ACKNOWLEDGEMENTS

cover page. I thank you for being open to Autistic lived experience, and dearly hope that you will continue your allyship by challenging the ableism that disables us. Thank you for making change happen; it starts with us!

One totally grateful Autistic, Jane McNeice x

Contact Me

If you would like to get in touch with me, here's how:

www.mindmatterstraining.co.uk

www.umbrellapicker.co.uk

Email: hello@umbrellapicker.co.uk

LinkedIn: Jane McNeice

Endnotes

1. 'Part 7: CBT for Cognitive Distortions' Cognitive Behavioural Therapy Los Angeles (2020) [online] Available from: https://cogbtherapy.com/cbt-for-cognitive-distortions [Accessed 25th August 2023]
2. Froreich FV, Vartanian LR, Grisham JR, Touyz SW. Dimensions of control and their relation to disordered eating behaviours and obsessive-compulsive symptoms. J Eat Disord. 2016 May 3;4:14. doi: 10.1186/s40337-016-0104-4. PMID: 27144009; PMCID: PMC4853853.
3. Megan E. (2021) 'Understanding Disordered Eating Risks in Patients with Gastrointestinal Problems' in Journal of the Academy of Nutrition & Dietetics. 2021. chrome-extension://efaidnbmnnnibpcajpcglclefindmkaj/https://eatrightmich.org/wp-content/media/Understanding-Disordered-Eating-Risks-in-GI-pts.pdf
4. Adamson J, Brede J, Babb C, Serpell L, Jones CRG, Fox J, Mandy W. Towards identifying a method of screening for autism amongst women with restrictive eating disorders. Eur Eat Disord Rev. 2022 Sep;30(5):592-603. doi: 10.1002/erv.2918. Epub 2022

Jul 5. PMID: 35791612; PMCID: PMC9540024.
5   Megan E. (2021) 'Understanding Disordered Eating Risks in Patients with Gastrointestinal Problems' in Journal of the Academy of Nutrition & Dietetics. 2021. chrome-extension://efaidnbmnnnibpcajpcglclefindmkaj/https://eatrightmich.org/wp-content/media/Understanding-Disordered-Eating-Risks-in-GI-pts.pdf
6   Raymaker, D.M., (no date) 'Autistic burnout: "My physical body and mind started to shut down" Available from: Academic Autism Spectrum Partnership in Research and Education (AASPIRE) [online] Available from: chrome-extension://efaidnbmnnnibpcajpcglclefindmkaj/https://www.seattlechildrens.org/globalassets/documents/health-and-safety/autism/autism_206_raymaker_slides.pdf
7   Dr Engelbrecht ND RP & Dr.Bercovici PhD 'It's not BPD, it's Autism' (2023) Embrace Autism [online] Available from: https://embrace-autism.com/its-not-bpd-its-autism/#References [Accessed: 25th August 2023]
8   Sandin S, Lichtenstein P, Kuja-Halkola R, Hultman C, Larsson H, Reichenberg A. The Heritability of Autism Spectrum Disorder. JAMA. 2017 Sep 26;318(12):1182-1184. doi: 10.1001/jama.2017.12141. PMID: 28973605; PMCID: PMC5818813.
9   Silberman, S. (2015) *Neurotribes: The Legacy of Autism and the Future of Neurodiversity* (Avery, New York)
10 Ibid

11 Rabiee A, Vasaghi-Gharamaleki B, Samadi SA, Amiri-Shavaki Y, Alaghband-Rad J. Working Memory Deficits and its Relationship to Autism Spectrum Disorders. Iran J Med Sci. 2020 Mar;45(2):100-109. doi: 10.30476/IJMS.2019.45315. PMID: 32210486; PMCID: PMC7071553.
12 Overton, G.L., Marsà-Sambola, F., Martin, R. et al. Understanding the Self-identification of Autism in Adults: a Scoping Review. *Rev J Autism Dev Disord* (2023). Available from: https://doi.org/10.1007/s40489-023-00361-x [Accessed: 25th August 2023]
13 National Autistic Society (2021) 'New Shocking Data highlights the Autistic Employment Gap' [online] Available from: https://www.autism.org.uk/what-we-do/news/new-data-on-the-autism-employment-gap [Accessed: 25th August 2023]
14 Sandin S, Lichtenstein P, Kuja-Halkola R, Hultman C, Larsson H, Reichenberg A. The Heritability of Autism Spectrum Disorder. JAMA. 2017 Sep 26;318(12):1182-1184. doi: 10.1001/jama.2017.12141. PMID: 28973605; PMCID: PMC5818813.
15 Baron-Cohen, S. (2020, 7th Edition) *The Pattern Seekers: How Autism Drives Human Invention* (First edition) Basic Books
16 National Institute for Health and Care Excellence 'Autism spectrum disorder in adults: diagnosis and management' Clinical guideline [CG142] Published: 27th June 2012 Last updated: 14th June 2021
17 Fern Brady (2023) "There's Not Enough Talk

On How Weird Neurotypicals Are." Fern Brady Discusses Autism. Channel 4, The Last Leg. March 2023. Available from: https://www.youtube.com/watch?v=HaqsScc32nQ [Accessed: 25th August 2023]

18 Cassidy, S, et al. Autism and autistic traits in those who died by suicide in England. BJPsych; 15 Feb 2022; DOI: 10.1192/bjp.2022.21

19 Ohlsson Gotby V, Lichtenstein P, Långström N, Pettersson E. Childhood neurodevelopmental disorders and risk of coercive sexual victimization in childhood and adolescence – a population-based prospective twin study. J Child Psychol Psychiatry. 2018 Sep;59(9):957-965. doi: 10.1111/jcpp.12884. Epub 2018 Mar 23. PMID: 29570782.

20 National Autistic Society (2023) 'Diagnostic Criteria – a guide for all audiences' [online] https://www.autism.org.uk/advice-and-guidance/topics/diagnosis/diagnostic-criteria/all-audiences

21 Young S, Moss D, Sedgwick O, Fridman M, Hodgkins P. A meta-analysis of the prevalence of attention deficit hyperactivity disorder in incarcerated populations. Psychol Med. 2015 Jan;45(2):247-58. doi: 10.1017/S0033291714000762. Epub 2014 Apr 7. PMID: 25066071; PMCID: PMC4301200.

22 The Equality Act 2010

23 Centre for Disability, 2023 [online] Available from: https://cdrnys.org/blog/uncategorized/ableism/ [Accessed: 25th August 2023]

24 Incredible Pianist Lucy Stuns Leeds Railway Station

| The Piano | Channel 4 [online] Accessible from: https://www.youtube.com/watch?v=nFWZbteCN2Q [Accessed 27th August 2023]
25 Cohen P, Cohen J. The clinician's illusion. Arch Gen Psychiatry. 1984 Dec;41(12):1178-82. doi: 10.1001/archpsyc.1984.01790230064010. PMID: 6334503.
26 Overton, G.L., Marsà-Sambola, F., Martin, R. *et al.* Understanding the Self-identification of Autism in Adults: a Scoping Review. *Rev J Autism Dev Disord* (2023). Available from: https://doi.org/10.1007/s40489-023-00361-x [Accessed: 25th August 2023]
27 Jeffers, S. (2007) *Feel the Fear and Do It Anyway*, Vermilion
28 Warrier, V., Greenberg, D.M., Weir, E. *et al.* Elevated rates of autism, other neurodevelopmental and psychiatric diagnoses, and autistic traits in transgender and gender-diverse individuals. *Nat Commun* **11**, 3959 (2020). Available from: https://doi.org/10.1038/s41467-020-17794-1 [Accessed: 25th August 2023]
29 Yipp, Ethan (2022) Beauhurst, 'Startup Fail, Scale & Exit Rates in the UK [online] Available from: https://www.beauhurst.com/blog/startup-fail-scale-exit/ [Accessed: 25th August 2023]
30 Running with Grit (2021) 'Statistics About Running; Runners Statistics; Running Facts' [online] Available from: https://runningwithgrit.com/statistics-about-running/ [Accessed: 25th August 2023]
31 Kendra Cherry, reviewed by Huma Sheikh (2021) Very Well Mind 'What are Alpha Brain

Waves?' [online] Available from: https://www.verywellmind.com/what-are-alpha-brain-waves-5113721#:~:text=Alpha%20waves%2C%20which%20measure%20between,during%20most%20conscious%2C%20waking%20states [Accessed: 25th August 2023]

32. National Institute for Health and Care Excellence. Alpha-Stim AID for anxiety disorders. Medical technologies guidance [MTG56] Published 8th March 2021. Available from: https://www.nice.org.uk/guidance/mtg56 [Accessed: 25th August 2023]

33. Lai, C. L. E., Lau, Z., Lui, S. S., Lok, E., Tam, V., Chan, Q., … & Cheung, E. F. (2017) Meta-analysis of neuropsychological measures of executive functioning in children and adolescents with high-functioning autism spectrum disorder. Autism Research, 10(5), 911-939

34. Mahony, James (2023) JPMorgan 'How our Autism at Work Program is Helping to Win the War on Top Talent [online] Available from: https://resources.vercida.com/jpmorgan-autism-at-work [Accessed: 25th August 2023]

35. National Autistic Society (2018) 'The Double Empathy Problem' [online] Available from: https://www.autism.org.uk/advice-and-guidance/professional-practice/double-empathy [Accessed: 25th August 2023]

36. Baron-Cohen, S. (2020, 7th Edition) *The Pattern Seekers: How Autism Drives Human Invention* (First edition) Basic Books

37 ibid
38 Mandavilli, Apoorva (2015) Spectrum News: 'The Lost Girls' [online] Available from: https://www.spectrumnews.org/features/deep-dive/the-lost-girls/ [Accessed: 25th August 2023]
39 Livingston LA, Colvert E; Social Relationships Study Team; Bolton P, Happé F. Good social skills despite poor theory of mind: exploring compensation in autism spectrum disorder. J Child Psychol Psychiatry. 2019 Jan;60(1):102-110. doi: 10.1111/jcpp.12886. Epub 2018 Mar 26. PMID: 29582425; PMCID: PMC6334505
40 Cherry, Kendra, Reviewed by David Susman Phd (2023) Mere Exposure Effect: How familiarity breeds attraction. Very Well Mind [online] Available from: https://www.verywellmind.com/mere-exposure-effect-7368184#:~:text=Exposure%20Reduces%20Uncertainty,less%20threatening%20and%20anxiety%2Dprovoking [Accessed: 25th August 2023]
41 Raymaker, Dora (2022) Understanding Autistic Burnout. National Autistic Society [online] Available from: https://www.autism.org.uk/advice-and-guidance/professional-practice/autistic-burnout#:~:text=Autistic%20burnout%20is%20a%20syndrome,and%20reduced%20tolerance%20to%20stimulus [Accessed: 25th August 2023]
42 National Autistic Society (2018) 'The Double Empathy Problem' [online] Available from: https://www.autism.org.uk/advice-and-guidance/

professional-practice/double-empathy [Accessed: 25th August 2023]

43 Brabban & Turkington (2002) 'The Stress Bucket'. Mental Health UK [online] Available from: https://mentalhealth-uk.org/blog/the-stress-bucket/ [Accessed: 25th August 2023]

44 International Classification of Diseases, Eleventh Revision (ICD-11), World Health Organization (WHO) 2019/2021 Available from: https://icd.who.int/browse11/l-m/en#/http://id.who.int/icd/entity/129180281 [Accessed: 25th August 2023]

45 Dora Raymaker (2022) Understanding Autistic Burnout. National Autistic Society [online] Available from: https://www.autism.org.uk/advice-and-guidance/professional-practice/autistic-burnout#:~:text=Autistic%20burnout%20is%20a%20syndrome,and%20reduced%20tolerance%20to%20stimulus [Accessed: 25th August 2023]

46 Weiss JA, Fardella MA. Victimization and Perpetration Experiences of Adults With Autism. Front Psychiatry. 2018 May 25;9:203. doi: 10.3389/fpsyt.2018.00203. PMID: 29887806; PMCID: PMC5980973. https://www.ncbi.nlm.nih.gov/pmc/articles/PMC5980973/

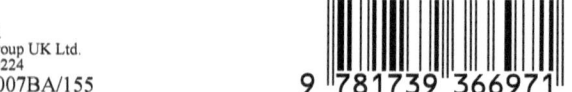